Adam's
Fractured
Rib

Observations on
Women in the Church

ADAM'S FRACTURED RIB

by
Margaret Sittler Ermarth

Cheerfully autographed!
Margaret S. Ermarth
Feb. 22, 1974

FORTRESS PRESS
Philadelphia

Library of Congress Catalog Card No. 78-117976

2725-B   Printed in U.S.A.   1-13

Contents

PART III
BASIC PROBLEMS OF EMANCIPATION

EXCERPTS

Foreword

A major part of the task committed by the Lutheran Church in America to its Commission on the Comprehensive Study of the Doctrine of the Ministry in 1966 was a study of the role of women in the life of the church, including the question of the ordination of women.

Mrs. Margaret Sittler Ermarth, professor of history at Wittenberg University, has headed a subcommittee of the commission entrusted with research into the whole problem of the role of women in the church. This book is a result of their labors over the past four years.

It is the hope of the commission that full discussion of this problem will ensue throughout the church. This book will help immeasurably in informing these discussions both from the viewpoint of the role of women in contemporary society and from the viewpoint of what has actually been going on in a number of church bodies including our own with respect to the activities of women in their life and work.

We commend this perceptive, informative, and lively study to all individuals and groups who want to approach the problem with open and informed minds.

EDMUND A. STEIMLE

Chairman of the Commission on the Comprehensive Study of the Doctrine of the Ministry of the Lutheran Church in America

Preface

The title of this book was chosen with some delight, to be sure, but also with utter seriousness. It states the message succinctly: whenever a member of a body is injured, the whole body suffers—whether it be the body politic, social, economic, or religious. During these years when segment after segment of our contemporary society is searching for a fuller participation, a richer experience, a truer identity, an escape from the strictures of the banal and the unproductive, women, too, are beginning to reexamine their role in society and in its institutions. Experience indicates, however, that when the status of womankind comes up for review, stalwart men blanch, anxious women recoil, and much of society reacts with a nervous chill. Therefore it would seem the better part of wisdom to reassure our readers as to the content and intent of this document. The book does, indeed, attempt to make clear how the current revolutions in society affect women and are affected by women—including specifically women of the churches. But it is not a polemic. It attempts to provide information that will help church people enter upon the discussion of an urgent matter fully aware that the attendant problems are complicated and touch upon many fundamental concerns and that "final and definitive" solutions probably will not be found.

All but the most obtuse or indifferent Christians are aware that their churches along with other institutions of our day are being buffeted about on a sea of revolutions and that the search for new formulations and structures through which the people of God respond to his will must go forward. What is not recognized generally, however, is that powerful currents involving half the human race are running their own courses under, within, and even against the currents of the other revolts.

The women's liberation movement—a phrase now spelled with capital letters to designate one rather amorphous grouping of revolutionaries—is a fact of contemporary life. It has risen out of the digs of the radical left, the demure halls of convents, the slums of the black matriarchy, the split-level houses of suburbia, and remote villages in India. This discontent will not go away nor be stayed by doctrine, habit, or diversion. And the movement is growing in power not on the strength of the traditional struggle for "women's rights," nor under the leadership of strident feminists; it springs rather from the same sources that are forcing drastic changes in economic, political, and social structures throughout secular society all over the world. It springs fundamentally from the desperate search for a fuller freedom and a larger meaning in life for the individual in mass society and, especially, for new perspectives in man-woman relationships. It is true that the movement has its roots in the industrial and technological revolutions which first brought women out of the home and into the factory and office, and which paved the way for democratic equalitarianism and mass education. But its contemporary strength is gathered rather from the civil rights struggle, the depersonalization of mass societies, and the threat of annihilation of the human race.

The changes being wrought are profound, pervasive, and immediate, and they are filled with grave problems and enormous opportunities for the church. It is already too late for the church to exercise its onetime celebrated but recently unused genius for the role of pioneer, but it is not too late for it to respond to a volatile situation it inadvertently helped to create, does not fully comprehend, and seems, on the whole, reluctant to acknowledge. In other words, the church in its thinking and its action has lagged seriously behind secular society in trying to cope with the woman problem.

The point has now been reached where a responsible church has no choice but to participate in the debate and in the action. Rich resources for the unavoidable effort are to be found in the teachings of the church about creation and redemption, about baptism, rite as over against sacrament, the concept of vocation, the freedom of the Christian, the sacredness of individuality, ecumenism, and a new and dynamic concept of the ministries of the church.

Theologians of all churches are concerned with the manifold problems of contemporary life. But solutions for the woman problem are not easy to find. The Presbyterian church supported a seven-year study, and is still debating. The Anglican church has produced a brilliant literature but has not been able to make up its mind as to a course of action. The Lutheran Church in America ordered into existence its second Commission on the Comprehensive Study of the Doctrine of the Ministry at its annual convention in 1966. In connection with its broader task this commission was instructed specifically to examine women's role in the life of the church including the matter of ordination. This book is based upon the findings of a subcommittee whose formal report has been reviewed by the whole commission, but it does not necessarily represent the views of all members.

We see the effect of the women's liberation movement on the churches most dramatically in the Roman Catholic

Church. Some Protestant churches have allowed women to enter the preaching ministry; others are divided in opinion and practice; some forbid it. As for the women—particularly the religiously devoted, gifted, and professionally educated women—they have on the whole responded pragmatically to a confused and frustrating situation and have reflected little resentment or bitterness. They have in considerable numbers entered upon "ministries" outside the churches, where their abilities are more fully recognized and rewarded. The nonprofessional women who work for the churches are also reaching out for new directions and new functions; there is blind groping; there are brave experiments; and there *is* movement.

The problem of women in the life of the church is as old as the church. What is new is the element of urgency and certain obvious consequences of nonresponse. The problem can be faced and made an opportunity for grace, or it can be evaded or suppressed and be accounted a rejection of grace. In any event, it just could be that the Holy Spirit is trying to tell us something.

MARGARET SITTLER ERMARTH

Subcommittee on the Role of Women in the Life of the Church
  Margaret Sittler Ermarth, chairman
  Dr. Marianka Sasha Fousek
  Dr. Victor R. Gold
  Dr. Jacob W. Heikkinen
  Sister Anna Melville
  Dr. Alfred H. Stone

Acknowledgments

As the custodian of the materials and observations presented in this book, I assume responsibility for the selection of data and the form of presentation. Contributions made by individuals on the Subcommittee on the Role of Women in the Life of the Church are identified in the footnotes and here gratefully acknowledged. I also wish to thank Dr. Edmund A. Steimle, commission chairman, for kindly writing an introduction to this book, and I want to acknowledge the help, inspiration, and treasured fellowship of the entire commission.

Special thanks are due several persons not on the commission: to Patricia O'Connor for her research on the role of women in the Roman Catholic Church; to Carolyn Eiterman and Alicia Pfnister for keeping an eye on current developments reported in secular magazines, newspapers, and religious journals. I am profoundly grateful for the work of Frau Irmgard Meissner-Schulte, of Düsseldorf, Germany, a theologian and *Vikarin* and formerly assistant to Bishop Hans Lilje of the Church of Hannover. Frau Schulte reported on developments in the churches of Germany, both East and West. I thank Dr. Minnie Cate Morrell, professor of English at Wittenberg University, for reading a portion of the manuscript. I also acknowledge with gratitude the fact that Wittenberg sustained my efforts by allowing me to devote a considerable number of faculty working hours to this project, and I appreciate their employing the most helpful and gracious of librarians.

Lastly, I wish to recognize the poignant and profound insight of Mrs. Reva Dixon, a Christian who twice a week observes with a benevolent wonder the clutter of papers and books that marks the intellectual enterprise. When I tried to explain my project to her, she said simply, "Doesn't everybody know that a woman carried the Word around for nine months before the men could start preaching about him?" And then she took off to bake two hundred sweet-potato pies to sell for the Church of God in Christ—a congregation of forty-eight members—to support their mission work, a parable on perspective for the third and fourth centuries and for the twentieth.

Part I

The Issue
and Why
It Arose

Chapter 1

The
Contemporary
Scene

It is obvious that the human race is at a critical turning point in its history—a turning point that is accurately called revolutionary. It is also generally recognized that in the midst of this revolution the human race looks toward its future with grave misgivings fed by its ignorance about how we arrived at our present condition and about the character of the drastic changes we are experiencing. We are enslaved by feelings of confusion and helplessness in facing our awesome future.

Society is working out new roles for men and women in their vocations, social life, sex life, and family life. In Sweden, for instance, where preruns of social phenomena are often visible, the parliament is considering legislation that would make it possible for a father to shorten his working day so that he can be present at home to share the tasks and joys of the household in the same measure as his wife shares the support of the family in her work. Partnership, rather than the patriarchal structure that has been traditional in Western society for many centuries, seems to be emerging rapidly as a viable formula for the late twentieth century.

The role of women, who now constitute 53 percent of American society, is being discussed in literally hundreds of studies: by the President's Commission on the Status of

3

Women, by the United Nations, by the universities, by the World Council of Churches, by the National Council of the Churches of Christ, by many of the major denominations, and by national professional organizations. Organizations are coming into existence specifically to carry the banner for a fair deal for women in our society. Leading this group is NOW, the National Organization for Women, formed in the fall of 1966 ". . . to take action to bring women into full participation in the mainstream of American society NOW, exercising all the privileges and responsibilities thereof in truly equal partnership with men."[1]

"Despite all the talk about isolated gains made by women in recent years," NOW says in its invitation to the public to join its ranks, "the actual status of women in the United States has been *declining,* rather than advancing in the 1950s and 1960s. Although more than 46 percent of American adult women now work outside the home, the overwhelming majority—75 percent—are in routine clerical, sales, or factory jobs; or they are household workers, cleaning women, hospital attendants. Some two-thirds of Negro women workers are in the lowest paid service occupations. Working women are becoming increasingly concentrated on the bottom rungs of the job ladder."[2]

The amazing increase in the employment of women in secular society, usually looked upon as emancipation, has actually operated to lock them into subordinate strata of that society where they have not only been deprived of advancement but receive lower wages, fewer fringe benefits, and much less security than their male counterparts. They have settled for low-paying jobs, 75 percent of them toiling at routine tasks that pay them less than $5,000 a year; many make less than $3,000. In 1963, 9 percent of employed men, but only .6 percent of women, earned $10,000 a year or more.[3]

4

The ugly fact of discrimination plays a weighty role in the waste of talent that is now being publicly recognized. Presidents Kennedy and Johnson both acknowledged and made significant efforts to combat discrimination against women by giving their support to the enactment of the Civil Rights Act of 1964, whose Title VII finally prohibited discrimination in employment on the basis of sex as well as race, color, religion, and national origin, and the government's record is clearly superior to the records of business and the professions.[4] In 1965 the Harvard Business School conducted a poll of one thousand male executives to discover their attitudes toward women as executives. Eighty-two percent thought women possessed the necessary abilities to make valuable contributions. Only 33 percent were willing to hire them as executives. Only 11 percent thought that women actually had equal opportunity in their business. One case is so typical that a description of it in the victim's own words is instructive. We have here a woman of twenty-nine with a college degree in sociology and articulate in three languages:

When I came to New York . . . everybody said the way to break in was as a secretary. Well, I was the best damn secretary they had at one of the television networks for three years. Meanwhile, a boy who started out—as a page—when I did was already a unit manager. Another was a production assistant. When I asked about something like that for me, I was told, "Those are men's jobs." So I started answering ads that said unlimited opportunities for bright college girls, and all they wanted to know was how fast I could type.

The job I have now sounded great—research assistant to the vice-president. But as soon as they found out I'd been a secretary, they had me organizing things around the office. Everybody says I'm marvelous. . . . They just hired a man for $12,000 a year as a research assistant, and guess what—I'm supposed to show him the ropes.[5]

5

A larger number of women than ever before are going into occupations that are listed as professional, technical, etc., with seven professions claiming four out of every five women: teaching, nursing, music, social work, accounting, auditing, and library work. In professions not traditional for women, 6,600 women are engineers, 9,000 are bank officials, 1,000 hold high civil service positions, and about 150 are officers in the foreign service.[6] Whereas the number of professional women is rising, the *percentage* of professional women is steadily declining. *In 1930, 50 percent of women workers were classed as professional or semiprofessional; in 1960, less than 35 percent.*[7]

These statistics become especially meaningful in view of the fact (now commonly known and certainly to be applauded) that since World War II more and more men are entering professions traditionally "reserved" for women: teaching, social work, library science, dietetics, nutrition, and nursing. In 1960, there were, at long last, more men in high school teaching than women, and considerably more entering elementary education. Men, however, enter these professions at the top, and thus ". . . perpetuate the stereotype that leadership and administrative aptitude are not qualities found in gifted persons, but are the property of the male sex alone."[8]

This trend is all the more important in view of the increasing need in our society for professional services, which are now enlisting *twice* as many persons as before 1954. For example, there is a dire shortage of doctors, and yet a prejudice against women becoming doctors. A medical conference in 1968[9] reported four findings particularly revealing about the role of women: 1) "Career predilections are culturally determined and our culture conceives of medicine in terms of the male doctor";[10] 2) "There are two minority groups in medicine today—Negroes and women. The Negro woman faces the problem of belonging to a double minority group";[11] 3) There are "secret" quotas for women students in some medical schools, but these are beginning to break down;[12] 4) Women doctors are needed as *women*.[13]

WOMAN DOCTORS ARE NEEDED AS WOMEN

We need their influence in medical care for the sake of those characteristics which women have and which men lack. Medicine needs women to strengthen the profession's concern with the community and its multitude of health-related problems of poverty, lawlessness, crowding, and alienation. The public needs, in larger measure, the commitment which women physicians naturally have for all our children's problems, extending beyond physiologic disability into those social and psychological realms so often relegated by physicians to the nonmedical area.

American medicine has performed near miracles on the technical side; we have not done so well with other elements of our duty. I believe more women physicians could aid greatly in the human aspects of health care. They can help, not just to provide extra hands or substitutes for scarce men, but to bring attributes of concern, of empathy, of heart that often seem in short supply today. . . .

Today about 8 percent of applicants to medical schools are women; they are admitted in about the same proportion to applications as men. The problem is not one of unwillingness of medical schools to admit women, but, instead, of the small number of women who seek careers in medicine. Why so few?

Our students have one answer that comes through loudly and clearly. In many cases they have been discouraged by their parents, their teachers, their family doctor, and their college counselors. Why? Because in America today, "doctoring" is still generally considered to be a man's job.

We need to shout, from one end of the country to the other, that it is *right* for a young women to want to be a doctor. We need to say more, though; we need to say that women physicians, well trained and dedicated, provide something special to health care — special attributes over and above the additional numbers promised. This is the effective argument against the contention that women physicians are, educationally speaking, a nuisance — that they have a high dropout rate, that they are too mobile, that they spend much of their energies "nesting." The conviction that women physicians have something special to give will go far to convince medical school faculties and hospital administrators that a special effort to accommodate women is worthwhile.[14]

In scientific vocations generally women have been culturally brainwashed to stay out or get out. *On a percentage basis there are fewer women today engaged in scientific enterprises than thirty years ago.* A decade ago a prominent scientist referred to women as "the lost half." "The biological facts must be conceded; but other nations are making it clear that it is possible to make adjustment to these biological facts and give women full opportunity for creative careers in science. . . . As the pressure for able personnel increases, we simply must create new, appropriate opportunities for women."[15]

A similar reexamination of traditional views and patterns of work for women is taking place in academic callings, in which it was said, as of 1959, ". . . women scholars are not taken seriously and cannot look forward to a normal professional career . . . because they are outside the prestige system entirely."[16] The great and liberal University of Chicago, for instance, has just set up a committee to investigate overt and covert discrimination against its women faculty members. It is manifestly unfair that West Virginia has a state university for men only, that coeducational institutions commonly establish quotas of 60 percent men students and 40 percent women students, and that women applicants must be better prepared and have higher academic and other personal qualifications even to be considered. Since 1930, women have received a decreasing proportion of higher degrees as well as faculty appointments. One-fifth of women with four years of college education receive unskilled or semiskilled jobs, and 8 percent of women with five years of higher education are in the same category. *It is significant that none of the statistical studies that classify the occupations women enter after graduation even mentions church-related work as an occupation.*

Other areas of discrimination in the common life run from the radical left, for example, the Students for a Democratic Society, to credit unions;[17] they include advertisements for employment in the daily newspapers and the general absence of any accounts in textbooks of the contribution of women to our national life. The woman takes her place in the limbo of the forgotten along with the Negro and the Indian.

Now, before paranoia sets in among the women readers, and the hackles rise threateningly on the men, remember that both men and women have been programmed by society to create and sustain the situation. The current waste of a great human resource is partly the result of women having *accepted* the psychology of a minority. They feel discriminated against and think as if inferiors of the second sex.[18] It is the woman's image of herself, as well as gross discrimination in a male-dominated society, that has contributed to the waste.[19] Our society is experiencing this "hang-up" in every aspect of the common life—the Establishment, the hippies, and the churches. The core of the demands of the new movement for the liberation of women

9

is a recognition by society of women and men as *persons* so free that their very masculinity and femininity, usually accepted automatically as a proper dividing line within the myriad activities and interests of society in any given era, may instead be celebrated as providing a new and creative partnership in a new age that is increasingly demanding a respect for individual freedom along with community of thought and action. "Equality" is not the key word any more; "brotherhood," "community," is. The enormous potentiality of this concept not only for individuals, but also for society in general, for the family, and for the church gives force, poignancy, and hope for a creative response.

Meanwhile, the Christian church has lagged behind the secular world in imagination, inventiveness, and daring. The ministry of women in a professional sense in modern times has not been brought into the mainstream of the life of the church, nor has the ministry of women kept pace with (not to speak of setting the pace for) the new role of

---

A TIME OF TRANSITION

Conventional patterns identify the man as provider and the woman as homemaker. When these lines blur, a period of readjustment is required until the cultural transition is completed. Such a transition is now going on. Times have changed but the image of the roles of men and women have not kept pace even among those whose education has kept up-to-date with new ideas. . . . The important fact we need to know is that we are not acting upon the facts we have, but rather we continue to act on the stereotypes which available facts have, in numerous instances, already disproved. The best minds of those persons most dedicated to the problems of the woman are held, almost by hypnotic compulsion, to a re-search for facts already known.[20]

---

women and the new possibilities open to them in modern Western society. Paradoxically, the church, steadily supportive of a basic patriarchal structure, has pioneered in women's education and has taught a concept of Christian love that has led women to break the cake of custom and enter professions such as teaching, nursing, and social service. Yet at the same time the church has frustrated them by denying them the rewards of full professional status.

Could it be that the development of the primarily local, parish-centered concept of the church is to blame? Could it be that the greater variety of ministries demanded of the church in our day by a predominantly city culture will once more call upon the gifts that women once exercised within the church? This is not to suggest that we need to have in our day any specifically female ministries, but rather that where a variety of the Spirit's gifts and services are appreciated in the church's ministerial structure, the gifts of the Spirit to a woman may be more readily acceptable. It is not an accident that women were allowed to prophesy and pray as the Spirit moved them in the primitive church as well as in the sects—for where the accent is on the Spirit and his gifts, he cannot be muffled or channeled into conventional forms.

NOTES

1. From a mimeographed sheet distributed by NOW. No date.
2. Ibid.
3. U.S. Department of Commerce, Bureau of the Census, *Statistical Abstract of the United States, 1965*, p. 346.
4. President Nixon apparently is making a valiant effort. The White House has made public a list of thirty-five women appointed or reappointed by the President among the fifteen hundred executive positions to be filled. Fifteen of the thirty-five named to commissions, committees, or boards were on a part-time consultant basis. One woman was named assistant secretary of Health, Education, and Welfare. One was named ambassador to Barbados.

5. Marilyn Mercer, "Women at Work: Is There Room at the Top?" *Saturday Evening Post,* July 27, 1968, p. 17.

6. Ethel J. Alpenfels, "Women in the Professional World," in Beverly Benner Cassara, ed., *American Women,* p. 73.

7. Ibid., p. 74.

8. Ibid., p. 76.

9. Conference on Meeting Medical Manpower Needs, sponsored by the American Medical Women's Association, the President's Study Group on Careers for Women, and the Women's Bureau of the U.S. Department of Labor, held in Washington, D.C., in 1968.

10. Report of the Conference on Meeting Medical Manpower Needs, *The Fuller Utilization of the Woman Physician* (Washington, D.C.: Woman's Bureau of the Department of Labor, 1968), p. 8.

11. Ibid., p. 45.

12. Ibid., p. 46.

13. Ibid., p. 75.

14. Ibid., pp. 75-76.

15. Warren Weaver, "A Great Age for Science," in *Goals for Americans: The Report of the President's Commission on National Goals* (New York: Prentice-Hall, Spectrum Book, 1960), pp. 115-116.

16. Theodore Caplow and Reece J. McGee, *The Academic Marketplace* (New York: Basic Books, 1958), pp. 111, 226.

17. Paula Stern, "When's It Going to Be Ladies' Day?" *New Republic,* July 5, 1969, pp. 14-15.

18. On the very startling and controversial psychological and social consequences of the relegating of women to a passive role in sex for instance, for which the author blames the traditional stance of the Judeo-Christian influence, see Laurence James Ludovici, *The Final Inequality.*

19. On the problem of image-making and image-acceptance, see the excellent books by Martin Gruberg, Peggy Lamson, Edwin C. Lewis, and Caroline Bird with Sara Welles Briller, listed in the bibliography.

20. Alpenfels, "Women at Work," in Cassara, ed., *American Women,* p. 85.

Chapter 2

How
Did We
Get Here?

For two thousand years the church has preached knowledge, faith, hope, and love as the ingredients of a creative response to life and it is in this tradition that this book now addresses itself to the task of illuminating the present by examining the shape of the experience in history of one-half the human race—the women. We want to point out the essentially religious nature of the question and the responsibility of the church to undertake anew a careful and faithful review of its stance.

In primitive society, man's survival depended upon, among other things, an increasingly sophisticated division of labor. While her mate hunted and fought off predators, the female nurtured and protected the young and tended the fire. There was basic equality built into the brutal struggle to live. But the position of women in some early societies changed as man gave thought to the mysteries of life. Men came to look upon women as possessing magic and occult powers because of their ability to produce children. (Some societies apparently saw no connection between sexual intercourse and the birth of an infant nine months later.) The regular issue of blood that corresponded to the phases of the moon seemed a "sign" of occult power also, for blood was to almost all societies the basic sign of vitality and of existence itself. And so the association of *fire, fertility,* and *woman* provided the focal point for early religious rites and ceremonies. Woman became the mother-goddess of earthly bounty, the symbol for life itself, and a means of seeking relief from hardship and danger. The cult of Isis, for instance, spread rapidly throughout the Mediterranean area, and temple prostitution became an official institution for the benefit of society. In important ancient civilizations, women also had vital property rights and other legal rights and enjoyed considerable freedom.

The ancient Jews, who fought continuously for their existence as a political, economic, social, and ethnic unity, reacted strongly against the alien and frequently inimical cultures around them. Still a primitive people and very much on the defensive, they eventually developed a patriarchal society with a sex code which reflected not only their rejection of the customs of the alien societies around them, but also the disciplined, male-dominated authoritarianism thought necessary to survival. Yahweh, the tribal God of the Jews and unique to them at this point, would bring vengeance upon the entire people for violations against religious purity. Hosea and Isaiah in the eighth century B.C., and Ezekiel and Jeremiah during the time of the Babylonian Exile, in the sixth century B.C., thundered against association with alien gods and the cults involving religious prostitution associated with them. It was during the Exilic period and Judaism's contact with the Babylonian matriarchal society that the later Jewish conceptions of women and sex were more rigidly drawn.

These conceptions are reflected in the laws found in the Book of Leviticus, which tends to view sex as unclean. Since women are sex symbols, these laws are not only antisex but antifeminine. Women came to be regarded as temptresses and political traitors to the security of the Chosen People. Sexual intercourse came to be looked upon as basically unclean. A man had to purify himself by washing before he went to worship before the Jewish tribal deity. After giving birth to a male child a woman was "unclean" for seven days, and a period of thirty-three days was required for her purification; the birth of a female child rendered her unclean for fourteen days, and required sixty-six days for purification. The daughters of priests could be burned at the stake for violating the code and thus interfering with their father's vocations. Leviticus contains a list of heavy penalties imposed against violators of women, who were looked upon as property—first of the father, then of the husband. Adultery (which violated property rights) was punishable by death. The legends, laws, and literature of the Jews also carry a common notion that sexual intercourse weakens a man. The Book of Proverbs bears this out. Daughters who resisted the stern regulations were the subject of many barbs from a second century B.C. writer, Ecclesiasticus: "From garments flieth out moths and from women wickedness." "I found more bitter than death the woman whose heart is snares and nets, and whose hands are fetters, he who pleases God escapes her. . . ." "Women are overcome by the spirit of fornication more than men and in their hearts they plot against men."[1] In short, the necessity to survive as a nation and as the practitioners of a unique and exclusive monotheistic religion helped to shape a dark tradition which fastened upon women the burden of constraint and selective contempt.[2]

This whole tradition represents what we might call, with a reasonable amount of historical understanding, and with *great* restraint, the "Eve Syndrome." In the mind of the ordinary person the story goes somewhat like this: when after the creation the Lord God went looking for Adam and Eve in the Garden of Eden, he asked first, "Where are you?" and second, "How did you get in this sorry state?" Then he made his judgment in no uncertain terms upon the serpent, upon Eve, and finally upon Adam (apparently moving up the ladder). The serpent was compelled forever to crawl upon his belly; the woman was to bring forth her children in much travail and to be ruled by her husband; Adam was to earn his bread by the sweat of his brow. All three were expelled from paradise. No matter how one reads this story of the fall of man from grace, it is pretty grim.

Given the influence of the Bible over the millennia one can understand why snakes are anathema, why women have been deemed temptresses and prone to do the devil's business, and why Eve, created from Adam's rib as an after-thought and now held responsible for his fall, has been considered his inferior. Two things only are to be wondered at: that Adam's lame excuse in the garden ("The woman whom thou gavest to be with me, she gave me fruit of the tree, and I ate") has never jeopardized his primary position, and, second, that arguments against women's full participation in the life of the church are still derived from a simplistic and literal interpretation of Genesis. Again, scholars and theologians can explain and explain, yet after two thousand years the basic image has not changed. The position of woman *after* the fall has been taken as the normative one rather than her position in creation where God is said to have created male and female, presumably on a par with each other, especially according to Genesis 1, which in other aspects of theology has dominated the church's notion of creation.

Jesus did not say much about women. His views were expressed primarily in his actions, and these actions constituted a dramatic breakthrough within that society whose dismal views on the female and on sex have been pointed out. Using the concept of the new creation as over against the old creation, Dr. Conrad Bergendorff summarizes this significance of Jesus' ministry regarding women:

> Christ nowhere distinguishes between men and women as children of God and objects of his redemptive ministry. Women are present from the Annunciation to the Ascension, and Mary, Martha, [and] Magdalene are as important in the Gospels as Peter, James, or John. He discourses with the woman at the well, he heals women, he includes them in his parables. When the Sadducees (Matthew 22) seek to snare him on a question of the relationship of husband and wife in the Resurrection, he does say that in the resurrection state there is no giving or receiving in marriage, but he does not say that man will have any pre-eminence over women. Indeed one finds nowhere that Jesus ranks man and woman. He treats each as an individual per se. The only pre-eminence he allows is that of service, "Whosoever would be first among you shall be your servant" (Matt. 20:27). By the regard he shows to women, by the treatment he gives them in word and act, by the purity and universality of his love and ministry, Jesus Christ erased all lines of superiority or inferiority between men and women and placed all on the same level of grace.[3]

Not even St. Paul was able consistently to realize the meaning of this new order. He too was a child of his times, a former Pharisee who had been brought up in the strict views of Judaism and who as the apostle to the Gentiles saw the evidences of a freedom in the Greek cities which to him seemed to be license. Offended by these excesses, practiced among the congregations even at worship, Paul seems to have forgotten his own lofty statement made to the Galatians that "there is neither Jew nor Greek, there is neither slave nor free, there is neither male nor female; for you are all one in Christ Jesus" (Gal. 3:28). Instead, with an emphasis on the authority of Christ, he sets up a hierarchy, stating, "But I want you to understand that the head of every man is Christ, the head of the woman is her husband, and the head of Christ is God" (I Cor. 11:3). Then he argues for women's cutting off their long hair or wearing veils during public worship. His basis for this position has long been disputed by scholars because his reasoning is by no means clear. What is clear is that he was dealing with the specific problems in the Corinthian congregation in terms of the culture of his day, both Jewish and Greek.[4] Except for the hierarchy of man-Christ-God, Paul was not speaking here in terms of his own understanding of the position of all believers in Christ, which he maintains elsewhere in the Corinthian Epistles as well as in the Epistles to the Galatians and Romans. Is it not interesting that the churches ever since should have made his conditional statement into an absolute for all times and all places, whereas his universal statement that all are one in Christ should be neglected in this context?

But, pressed as he was, not even Paul was as stringent or as fanatic as the church fathers who came after him. Origen identified the body as evil and advocated castration as a way to avoid the temptations of women. Ambrose applauded virginity and suggested that widows not remarry. Augustine's youthful passions, which he belabors extensively in the *Confessions,* his Manichaeism, and finally his Christian view of the nature of evil all conspire to concentrate upon the carnal. The weight of Augustine's views in the development of Christian theology is very great indeed, and that weight has rested heavily upon the female of the species. And so the Eve Syndrome lived on in spite of the new creation in Christ, which only underscores the truly revolutionary nature of Jesus' treatment of women and the situation in the early church in which for a brief time women who were Christians participated significantly.

There was a great variety of ministries in the early church in which women served.[5] But only one of these ministries, that of the "widow" (I Tim. 5:3-16), was institutionalized. Their work was of a charismatic nature; they taught, prophesied, prayed in the congregation, and assisted in missionary work. The variety of names assigned to them differed with the services they performed, the place where they served, and the times. They were called "widows," "deaconesses," and "virgins," but their duties and privileges were not always clearly defined. Slowly the charismatic ministries in general dried up, were suppressed, or came under stricter surveillance (institutionalized) because of the rising fear in the early church of heretical teaching that would destroy the apostolic tradition. Restrictions laid upon the participation of women in public worship are to be understood in the light of this fear and in light of the restrictions laid upon women by other institutions in the society of that time.

Two distinctive features of the organization of the ancient church made it possible for women to render notable services (ministries) to the very early church. In the first place, a whole city constituted a parish. Variety and flexibility were indispensable. Teams of Christians working together performed a great variety of the services (*diakoniōn*). There was no such thing as *the* ministry. The ministries responded to the needs of the church and the gifts of the ministers as Paul enumerated them in I Corinthians. This variety persisted throughout the ancient era even as the church structure stabilized. In the third century we find bishops, presbyters, deacons, deaconesses, lectors, acolytes (the bishops' trusted letter-carriers), exorcists, and "doorkeepers." Each office had its own dignity and importance, but the individual offices were not yet seen as steppingstones toward some "higher" position. The "ladder" concept—one climbs up to "higher office" by means of "lower offices"—emerged as the church began to reflect the civil service system of the Roman Empire.

Under the impact of the barbarian invasions into Western Europe, society ceased to be urban-centered. "Grass
grew in the streets of Rome" as people fled or drifted into
the countryside. The population of the West became rural,
and the "local parish" as we know it found its basic form
under the circumstances of life in the early Middle Ages.
The break-up of the city-wide parish also spelled the inevitable break-up of the team ministry in practice, each
country parish now simply being served by one minister,
the presbyter (priest), even though he was still responsible
to the (now distant) bishop. A team ministry remained
only in the bishop's place of residence, where the clergy
when they were unmarried (the *canon* presbyters and the
"apprentices" to the presbyterate, and, in the East, also the
life-deacon) resided with the bishop in a semimonastic
community. There was little place for women in this situation, but the ministerial women had already been safely
tucked away in the cloister, which sheltered them and also
as an institution took over most of the ministerial functions
the ecclesiastical women had exercised in the ancient
church.

Because some of us are unprepared to understand arguments about the role of women and ordination based on
tradition, it is important here to undertake a somewhat
detailed account of the origins and fate of various "offices"
women have occupied in the history of the church. The
"mother form" of the official (institutionalized) ministry of
women seems to have been the order of ecclesiastical
widows. In the third century the *diaconal* ministry of
women was institutionalized and defined, at least in the
Eastern part of the church. There the diaconal office slowly
absorbed and eclipsed the ministry and honor of the widow.
This development coincided with a parallel definition of
the office of the deacon. Both the deacon and deaconess

(or widow) functioned as a link between the bishop and his congregation; they were his ministers (literally "servants," which is what the word *diakon* means) in the service of the needy and in liturgical functions.

The widow and the deaconess were sometimes "instituted," sometimes "ordained" for their ministry. Their functions varied, but tended to be confined to caring for the needy, the sick, and the strangers, and to doing for women what the deacon or presbyter could not very well do, at least not alone, for the sake of decorum, such as calling on women in their homes, or bringing them Communion when they were sick, instructing women catechumens, anointing their bodies in the baptismal rites, guiding young women and women converts in the Christian life, and overseeing and directing women in the Christian assembly. One of the widow's primary functions was the duty of prayer (which may have involved liturgical prayer—Daniélou); they were called the "altar" of God, whereas the deaconess was considered a "type" of the Holy Spirit (the bishop was a "type" of God the Father, the deacon a "type" of Christ). The widow and deaconess were often classed as "clergy" and had their places of honor in the church assembly with the rest of the clergy. The deaconess was either unmarried (a celibate) or a widow and thus free from family responsibilities. Like the widow, she was able to devote herself fully to the service of the church. The widows or deaconesses, together with the church's virgins (the protonun), came to form semimonastic communities, often living together near the bishop's church and the clergy's residence.

The monastic movement—a strong ascetic reaction within the Christian community to a popular and more secularized church—further isolated women both from danger and from their accustomed services. In the fourth century, the virgins of the church began to outshine the widows and in the process absorbed their ancient diaconal functions as well as their honor. The deaconess of the Eastern church survived longer than her Western sister, the widow, but eventually she also was absorbed by the monastic movement, becoming simply the head (abbess) of the women's monastic communities, with all the duties and privileges of a deaconess, including teaching and liturgical rights short of presiding over the celebration of the sacraments. These autonomous Christian communities provided for the medieval church and the world what the ecclesiastical women had provided for the church while they still participated in the life of the city congregation. In the course of the centuries, certain nuns enjoyed great authority. For instance, Hilda, abbess of Whitby, who presided over a synod in 664, Catherine of Siena, and St. Teresa of Avila.

It seems astounding and unfortunate that the Reformation did not provide any substitute for the services and leadership women had exercised as nuns, prioresses, and abbesses. Yet many of these women would have been eminently qualified for valuable service to the church and the world, as can certainly be seen by what humanistically educated women and the women's religious orders and societies created by the Catholic Reformation could and did do. The lack of organizational imagination on the part of the Lutheran Reformation is partly to blame. "The reformers of the sixteenth century, in suppressing the religious orders, deprived their churches of the only officially recognized form of women's service. The consequences of this for the diaconal work seem not to have been seriously studied by the reformers."[6] Even the Calvinist churches, with their recovery of the team ministry of the early church (elders, teachers, deacons), provided no place for a ministry of women. Only the "sects" had a role for women as prophets, teachers, and elders.

The Reformation emphasis upon the sanctity of the person, the rights and duties of the individual, and Luther's teaching about the priesthood of all believers, as well as the new humanism of the Renaissance and Enlightenment, all helped to lay the groundwork for the egalitarianism that swept over much of the Western world in the eighteenth century. This was the century of the American and French revolutions; in France and England, elegant and gifted women presided over fashionable salons and held court for intellectuals of the Enlightenment and the revolutionary period. In the society of colonial and revolutionary America women were free to work for society as it needed them as ". . . butchers, silversmiths, gunsmiths, upholsterers, jailkeepers, printers, apothecaries, and doctors. . . ."[7] The frontier used them and used them *up*, but they were not really free, legally, politically, socially, even though in the nineteenth century several frontier states gave women the vote—Wyoming in 1869, and, later in the century, Colorado, Utah, and Idaho.

The women were in motion, however, and in the nineteenth century under a few indefatigable leaders, whose names at least appear in high school textbooks in American history, a variety of women's movements sprang up, particularly before the Civil War, to better society by reforming prisons and asylums, founding hospitals and orphanages, and promoting education and securing basic rights for women. The strength of these movements, however, was siphoned off into antislavery movements. The Emancipation Proclamation technically brought personal, legal, and political freedom to the black man but not to women, black or white. For the right to vote women had to wait until 1920.

In the area of church work proper, the Pietists used the services of women in works of charity; later in the nineteenth century the order of deaconesses was created, and women also became active as Sunday school teachers and especially as missionaries.

The great emancipator for the masses, both men and women, was the Industrial Revolution, which, after an initial period of binding the lower classes of both sexes to unrelenting and grinding labor at the new machines for from sixteen to eighteen hours a day at pitiful wages, finally raised the standard of living for the great majority in the industrial nations of the world, and particularly in the United States. The effect on women was predictably bizarre, and the cost in terms of human life and dignity was great. The same revolution which created an elite class of monied bourgeois who could afford to support its women in high style as status symbols ("birds in a gilded cage" was the phrase used by the Victorians) had also condemned some of their sisters to crawl on hands and knees to move coal cars through the dark and wet tunnels of the British mines. Even those women who were "emancipated" from their homes to work in mill, factory, or behind the new typewriters and at telephone switchboards, or—particularly after the Civil War—behind the teachers' desks, were paid at roughly half the wages their male counterparts earned.

The first great leap forward for women in the economic life of the Western world came between 1900 and 1910. The pull of the office and the city, the "romantic accommodations" of the car and the telephone, worked inexorably to open the doors of the "gilded cage" as well as the doors of kitchen and nursery.[8] For the next generation no significant changes occurred, in spite of the noisy twenties and the Great Depression—the boom and bust period. Women were the last to be hired and the first to be fired. During World War I, women had begun entering the labor force in great numbers, thus filling the gap as a reserve labor force, which, in an earlier, rapidly growing industrial society, had been filled by slaves, children, and immigrants. They withdrew just as amiably after the Armistice in 1918 and again during the Depression of the thirties. The loosening up of manners, dress, and morals, however, continued apace.

World War II called women out to work in even greater numbers; this time they did *not* return home. Neither marriage nor children have inhibited the rise in the percentage of women employed outside their homes. In 1950, 14 percent of the mothers of *preschool* children worked; in 1960, 20 percent; in 1966, 26 percent. Today, women constitute about 40 percent of the labor force. Their labor and earnings are vital to the economy and, according to some economists, account for the current high level of American prosperity.[9] Economic facts alone have forced sociologists, psychologists, and moralists to reexamine their ideas about the nature of woman, her proper role in society, and basic man-woman relationships. The old clichés simply will not do. One cannot in the same breath blame juvenile delinquency on working mothers and call the culture "momistic." The data cannot be marshalled into a neat analysis or plan for action, but certainly it is clear that society is putting large numbers of women to work outside the home and that the options in their relationships with men are competition, suppression of one by the other, or a creative partnership.

NOTES

1. Biblical scholars and theologians will complain here that Semitic and Greek sources are mixed. But the Old Testament as a whole has left a strong impression that the subordination of women was an accepted tradition in our Judeo-Christian heritage. Much of the information in this section was provided by Dr. Cora Klick, associate professor of religion at Wittenberg University.

2. Because of the antifeminine viewpoint that had become dominant in Judaism in the centuries immediately before Christ, as well as in later orthodox Judaism, much of what the Old Testament says of the role of women in the earlier years of Israel's history tends to be forgotten. Best known, of course, are Sarah, Rebekah, and Hannah, each of whom had a profound influence as the mother of an important man in Israel. Less well known but equally significant is Deborah, the prophetess whose fame was such that a song was sung about her role in Israel's victory over some enemies. Hers was not a particularly feminine role. Nor was that of Jael, mentioned in the same song, who slew the opposing general and caused his army to flee. The politically significant women, e.g., Bathsheba, Jezebel, and Judith, may have used their feminine wiles to get their way, but that made their political influence not less but more. Note by Dr. Cora Klick.

3. "Man and Woman in the Old and New Creation," Appendix B in Elisabeth Hahn, *Partnership,* p. 62.

4. One explanation is that the message of the cross and the "foolishness of God" must not be obscured because women did not wear a veil or because they spoke up in public in a society where only prostitutes and courtesans did so. This was the law that was to be obeyed to keep the ears open to the real message of freedom under Christ in Gal. 3:28. "There is neither Jew nor Greek, there is neither slave nor free, there is neither male nor female; for you are all one in Christ Jesus." See Violette S. Lindbeck, "Should We Ordain Women?" pp. 18-24.

5. This paragraph and the next six paragraphs were written by Dr. Marianka Sasha Fousek, a member of the Commission on the Comprehensive Study of the Doctrine of the Ministry.

6. Madeleine Barot, *Cooperation of Men and Women in Church, Family and Society,* p. 33.

7. Bird with Briller, *Born Female,* p. 21.

8. James McGovern, "The American Woman's Pre-World War I Freedom in Manners and Morals," p. 319.

9. Of women between the ages of eighteen and twenty-four, 45 percent are employed, nearly one of every two; between the ages of twenty-five and thirty-four, 35 percent; between the ages of thirty-five and forty-four, 43 percent; between the ages of forty-five and sixty-four, 42 percent; over sixty-five years of age, 10 percent. These figures are based upon the 1960 United States census report and are quoted from Mary G. Roebling, "The Power and Influence of Women," *Vital Speeches,* vol. 31, September 1, 1965, p. 690.

Part II

Women in the Life of the Churches

Chapter 3

A General Look

The church means business when it announces that its most urgent ministry to contemporary man is to serve "the world" where the world needs the church. But many of its people, both clergy and laity, who are beginning to comprehend and to accept this fact, are nevertheless unprepared to grasp how significant to their task are the revolutionary changes that are taking place with regard to the role of women in secular and in religious life. Conventional thought about women, their traditional roles in society, in family life, in the man-woman relationship, and in the church is under fire from all sides.

In Part II of this book we want to try to convey some idea of what Christian women are doing in the churches, and how they view their work. The difficulties of presenting an accurate picture are formidable. In contrast to the secular segment of society, there are no census reports available on the work of women in the churches. For instance, the otherwise thorough and dependable *Monthly Labor Review* of the U.S. Department of Labor contained for the entire year of 1968 not one statistic or category that included women who were church workers or even parochial school teachers. Few researchers have been attracted to this apparently unspectacular aspect of the "woman problem." The first survey was authorized by the Federal Council of Churches in 1921. In 1969 the National Council of Churches sought information about the employment of women in professional or executive positions in the churches by addressing a questionnaire to 156 national boards and agencies. Of these, 65 units related to 17 denominations and the NCC itself responded. The statement summarizing the findings is revealing: ". . . these data reflect adherence to the rhetoric of equality of opportunity for women and men, on the one hand, and the factual conditions of considerable discrimination on the other." [1]

Our commission also attempted through a questionnaire to get some information from synodical offices of the Lutheran Church in America about attitudes toward women involved in professional work in the church, the numbers so employed, the experiences of these women in their work, etc. The results are important and interesting but the objective data do not surface and doubtless are unavailable.[2] One thing, however, is clear: concern about women in the contemporary church is very lively and is growing rapidly. A simple measure is provided by the fact that three-fourths of the items in our bibliography have become available since 1965. This concern is erupting into studies and rumors of studies being conducted by most of the major denominations. Those that have been made available reveal anxieties about the complexities of the problem, uncertainty as to the implications of their findings for the traditional work and structures of the churches, and all of them complain about the necessity for making decisions under the pressure of events within and outside the churches.

The next message that comes through is that the need of the churches for intelligent and well-trained manpower is growing by leaps and bounds, regardless of how its ministries are defined, just at the time many of its most able women are being absorbed into secular positions. Church positions simply do not attract women. However favorably they may be disposed toward their churches, most professionally educated women don't even think of their churches as potential employers. Nonchurch publications, for instance, designed to inform women college graduates about job opportunities mention no occupations in church-related work.

The relative barrenness of women's work in the secular life, marked by monotony, apathy, and frustration, even with a greater variety of opportunities available to them,

---

STEREOTYPES AND THE HEALTH OF THE CHURCH

Yet even those who believe in such stereotypes must be helped to recognize them as only partial truths which mask other realities and potentialities. For example, it is often forgotten that most women in the Church are not only sincerely motivated, but are *doing precisely that which Church leadership over the past fifty years has encouraged and provided opportunities for them to do.*

It is a fact that formal Church leadership (need we state that it is predominantly male?) has counted on the women to raise money *in whatever ways they could;* to do "good works" for *the entire Church;* and to keep themselves occupied in their own organizations and *out of the sessions, vestries, church councils, presbyteries, etc.-where the real decisions concerning the church are made.*

If women have honestly sought to do just this, then the words of the elderly woman who told me, "I don't understand — I've given my life to the circles, and now the new pastor tells us that they are all wrong" — are indeed plaintive.

Traditional women's groups are often branded as irrelevant, irreverent and banal. *But they are no more so than the rest of the Church* and the truth is that the struggles for renewal now going on within them bespeak of the latent health of the *entire* Body of Christ. . . .[3]

WOMAN'S SIN

Several years ago, a woman philosopher writing in the *Journal of Religion* suggested that theology tends to reflect masculine rather than feminine experience. And why not? Theologians are overwhelmingly men!

She also suggested that major theological emphasis upon pride as the condition for human sin reflects the traditional nature of male existence as embodying aggressiveness and power. False pride and the temptation to misuse power thus create the masculine condition for sinfulness, and the theological plea is for greater humility and less confidence in one's own resources.

The situation is different for women. The nature of feminine existence has traditionally been more passive and self-denying. Yet the theological plea has emphasized even greater humility and self-abnegation. Few — if any — have recognized that *too little pride, rather than too much pride, may be the condition of feminine sinfulness.*

It is not a far step to suggest that the banality of much women's work in the Church is related to such a dynamic. In their false pride, men tend to protect women from the "real world" and in women's lack of pride, they tend to accept this and retreat into "safe" roles. But if women do this, they must then accept the stereotyping, the condescending and sentimental view of their work held by many churchmen. And they are totally unprepared when a younger generation of Church leaders begins to look to them for programs of significance.

This dynamic affects all women in the Church. It is time to say openly that the Church treats its own professionally trained women, its Christian educators and pastors, as second class citizens. If this is so, it is no wonder that women's groups have followed the directions they have taken. The recently passed legislation assuring "equal pay for equal work" for women will be embarrassing to no organization more than the Church. But this is merely symbolic of the real gaps that exist between men and women Christians, whether in the various traditional ministries, or within the more recently emphasized ministry of the laity.[4]

is tragically pervasive in the church. In an incisive and shocking article in *Renewal* magazine, Peggy Way, formerly a social welfare consultant to the Chicago City Missionary Society, and now on the faculty of the Divinity School of the University of Chicago, describes trenchantly the stereotypes of "groups" of church women we all know too well. She calls them the bane of the minister, an impediment to *bona fide* church renewal, a breeding ground for self-satisfaction and contentment with the status quo, and an offense especially to active and intelligent young women of the church who are ". . . accustomed to the give and take of conversation in a bisexual environment . . . [and] less apt to seek out the sexually segregated 'proper' place for women which the church provides."[5] Tragically, these groups reveal the "latent health of the *entire* Body of Christ."

There are some bright spots in the picture, however. Despite the prevalent practice of keeping women "in their place" and out of decision-making groups, more and more women are being elected to local church councils and task forces and to national church bodies in all denominations (except, so far as we know, the Lutheran Church—Missouri Synod). Women also are taking major responsibility in executive positions in interchurch projects.[6] There is a new willingness to use enlightened literature and other materials for women's study groups and for devotional purposes. The impact of such improvements is difficult to measure except in one way: the young are obviously keeping their distance; the old stereotype of empty irrelevance, sentimental charity, and extreme conservatism still holds for them, and neither the young nor their elders are much impressed by numbers.

The familiar argument that men and women's roles are "complementary" leaves women not interested in traditional women's church groups cold. If roles are only complementary ". . . then both males and females are only half there when operating alone. . . . Actually, what happened in the churches was pretty much the experience of women in their community life also; in political parties and health and welfare organizations our responsibilities are limited by 'para-organizations' of a supporting nature." [7] These sentiments were voiced by representatives of Church Women United—a grass-roots movement in the United States pledged to maintain a maximum amount of flexibility and a minimum structure to ". . . find a responsible way to be God's instrument of reconciliation in a torn-apart world." [8] The CWU is ecumenical and interracial; it has task forces working on the problems of hunger, school dropouts, literacy, legislative reforms, and many proposals that affect women directly. CWU has programs for supporting a nurse in the Mississippi Delta ministry and for rehabilitating Indonesian war widows and victims of war in the Middle East. Support for international economic development is high on its agenda. This organization initiated and conducted a consultation on the Recruiting, Training, and Employing of Women Professional Church Workers in Greenwich, Connecticut, on February 26 and 27, 1969. The ecumenical activity of the CWU, which has enlisted a significant number of Roman Catholics, should be remembered when the debate over women's role in the church raises questions about the threat to ecumenism.

Shortly after World War II, when the Women's Section of the Lutheran World Federation met during the assembly in Hannover, Germany, to discuss theological questions involved in equal rights, it was the Swedish women who analyzed the sociological factors, the American women who contributed a wealth of material and a multiplicity of views which helped to identify practical tasks and aims, and the German women who, after discussions with theologians from all three countries, contributed the theological points of view.[9]

Outside the United States, the tradition of a nonfunctioning laity still largely holds. A lay stewardship program begun in Germany after World War II got off to a brave start, but it, too, presently suffers from the stubbornness of the "cake of custom." Interestingly enough, when European women break this cake of custom, which they do in considerable numbers, they do not usually choose to work within a congregation. If they are professional theologians they occasionally aspire to ordination, but usually they settle for teaching religion in the public schools. The diaconate is attracting fewer and fewer women in all areas where statistics are available.

Although the debate on women's role often, and regrettably, gets hung up on the problem of the ordination of women for the preaching ministry, the most profound consequences of the hesitant and often backward policies—or *lack* of policies—on the part of the church are to be found elsewhere. Women sociologists, psychologists, psychiatrists, doctors, economists, nutrition experts, teachers, etc., are lost to the church not only because they are not recognized as *ministering* in their vocations, but also because their salaries, retirement, security, and vacation arrangements and their titles of office simply do not indicate that their work as professionals is recognized. Even though many a woman would prefer to work for the church, she simply cannot afford to. Such a woman follows her male counterpart, including men trained for the pastoral ministry, *out* of the church and into society. The tragedy is that the loss comes precisely at a time when the church is redefining its concept of its ministries in the world of the ghetto, the suburbs, the underprivileged, the hungry, the aged, the have-not nations—the whole of our problem-ridden world—half of whose people are women.

The barrenness and irrelevancy of traditional forms of service for lay women in the local parishes have driven many able young women into the community to serve society on a voluntary basis. Their professionally trained sisters and other full-time women workers also find greater fulfillment in secular positions than in working for the church, even though in secular positions many of them enjoy less job security than does a Negro man. Women seem to be reacting to the same set of circumstances that influence a startling number of seminarians to reject or not to seek out positions within the parish. Prominent among these circumstances are certain traditional and conservative attitudes within the churches which seem to inhibit or blunt the new thrust of the church to involve itself in the great upheavals of our time.

NOTES

1. National Council of the Churches of Christ in the U.S.A., Department of Research, *Information Service,* vol. 48, no. 12 (May 31, 1969), p. 8.

2. See pp. 106-110.

3. Peggy Way, "Women in the Church," p. 5.

4. Ibid., pp. 7-8.

5. Ibid., pp. 4-5.

6. An American Woman, Mrs. Charlotte Proune-Mayers, member of the United Church of Christ, was provisionally appointed associate general secretary of the World Council of Churches and director of interchurch aid, refugee aid, and world service. She is the first woman to hold the position of associate general secretary. Two women before her have headed departments of the WCC.

7. Margaret Shannon, "CWU and the Women Liberators," p. 7. Margaret Shannon is the executive director of Church Women United.

8. Ibid.

9. Hahn, *Partnership,* pp. 2-3.

Chapter 4

In the Roman Catholic
and the Greek
Orthodox Churches

THE ROMAN CATHOLIC CHURCH

The turmoil within the Roman Catholic Church involving hierarchy and laity is rising rapidly, substantiating the widely-held judgment of students of revolution that where the lid has been held down longest and most firmly on a boiling cauldron of human frustrations, the greater will be the explosion. It would be hard to think of any aspect of the general turbulence that does not affect the women of the church in some way. The women know it, too. As one close observer wrote: "The emergence of the Catholic woman as a dynamic, often angry protester is perhaps the least recognized aspect of the current revolutionary ferment." [1] The long controversy over birth control, the declining attendance at mass (down 40 percent in Los Angeles in the winter and spring of 1968/69), the mushrooming of the "underground church"—now numbering from two thousand to three thousand groups in the United States alone, the attraction of the new "floating churches," officially permitted in 6 of 154 dioceses, the flood of priests leaving their priestly vocation, many of them to marry; the drastic decline in the number of Catholic women entering church vocations and obviously preferring VISTA or the Peace Corps to the uncertain values of convent life, the dignified revolt on the part of professional educators, artists, and writers among

Catholic women—all of these events and movements spell drastic changes. The resentment that found voice among Catholic women as a result of the single fact that the eminent British economist, Barbara Ward, a Catholic laywoman in the front rank of experts on worldwide poverty, had to sit silently at a meeting of the Vatican II discussants and listen while a man read her address is rather typical witness in the revolt of intellectuals and professionally-trained Catholic Christians.

Catholic women particularly, but also lay men and a goodly number of priests, look to the underground church movement as a source of the renewal Vatican II promised. It is a worldwide movement that has been active in France for more than fifteen years. In America the hierarchy is reluctant to experiment. Meanwhile the restive Catholic laity is building a reputation for contentiousness that threatens to put the Dutch Catholic church, long the record-holder, in second place. One Dutch priest-writer, Robert Allers, predicts a "blockbuster" explosion in America unless greater flexibility and imagination are used by the hierarchy in this country to meet the demands of the laity for freedom to participate.[2]

The need to experiment in social services, in education, and in liturgical procedures has led some nuns to discard their habits, their isolation, and their financial support from the church in order to establish themselves independently to work in the inner city and in the newly secularized Catholic institutions of learning. The National Council of Catholic Women solicited information from its membership on the extent to which women are now being allowed to participate in the liturgy. Women have lately been given permission by a decree of Vatican II to proclaim the lessons and Epistles at mass, but only if no male lectors are available and if they stand outside the presbyterium. And a woman theologian, a nun, president of a Catholic college, must still defer to an altar boy when the priest requires an acolyte at mass.[3]

The emergence of well-educated Catholic laymen into the whole service of the church *short of priesthood,* without regard to sex, is a phenomenon supported by Vatican II. Taking advantage of this position, many Catholic women who look for new levels and areas of participation have invested their interest in the Pentecostal movement, which strives to revive the traditions of the early church, emphasizes among both sexes the exercise of the Holy Spirit, the ability to speak in tongues and to prophesy, and supports an ecumenical spirit that overrides sex and any other factors that divide the Christian community.

A revolution of monumental proportions is occurring within convent walls and is symbolized by the shedding of the medieval habit. In accordance with the dictum of Vatican II, the nuns are redefining all aspects of their lives. In practice what this means at present is the assumption of real autonomy by the individual orders and democratization within the convent and the attempt to come to grips with the contemporary environment. While both of these points imply the realization of a new role for women within the church and will doubtlessly lead to more petitions for ecclesiastical office, the movement as a whole has not yet taken the latter direction. Some sisters, particularly those in mission work, would like to assume diaconal functions such as conducting services and distributing Holy Communion, but again, the priestly office of offering the sacrifice is not sought. Nuns are primarily searching for a more vital role in secular society and a more meaningful definition of their Christian apostolate. New communities of former nuns who have left their convents and their traditional garbs to serve in the hard-core areas of poverty have been formed in at least ten states. Most of them work in close cooperation with their bishops and must finance their own work. They aspire to more influence in decisions concerning the life of the religious, not in hierarchical decisions involving the church as a whole.

Nevertheless, the question of women assuming ecclesiastical office is under animated debate, to put it mildly. Modern popes have cautiously countenanced a more active social role for women, and since the church now readily admits that its understanding of "nature" is evolving in the light of modern psychological and biological discoveries, the label "natural" attached to a theory no longer relegates it to the realm of eternally settled questions. But canon law still restricts the valid reception of Holy Orders to *vir baptizatus,* a baptized male.

Mary Daly, a Catholic theologian in the United States and author of the striking and controversial book, *The Church and the Second Sex,* notes that a prominent Catholic dignitary, Msgr. J. D. Conway, writing in the *National Catholic Review,* November 16, 1966, had suggested that Pope John XXIII appeared to be ". . . opening just a crack the door to the priesthood for women, perhaps without realizing it, when he wrote in *Pacem in Terris: 'Human beings have the right to choose freely the state of life which they prefer, and therefore the right to establish a family, with equal rights and duties for man and woman, and also the right to follow a vocation to the priesthood or the religious life.'"* Then, after quoting this passage, Msgr. Conway commented further: "Pope John might object to my taking his words literally but they deserve meditation. He noted with approval the fading of a stratified society, in which some persons are put in an inferior condition, and others assume superior position, 'on account of economic and social conditions, of sex, of assigned rank.'" [4]

40

Miss Daly contends that a similar procedure might be used to interpret a passage from Vatican II's *Pastoral Constitution on the Church in the Modern World,* which declares all discrimination to be contrary to God's intent.

A CATHOLIC THEOLOGIAN'S ARGUMENT FOR ORDAINING WOMEN
The Pastoral Constitution Statement

"With respect to the fundamental rights of the person, every type of discrimination, whether social or cultural, whether based on sex, race, color, social condition, language, or religion, is to be overcome and eradicated as contrary to God's intent. For in truth it must still be regretted that fundamental personal rights are not yet being universally honored. Such is the case of a woman who is denied the right and freedom to choose a husband, to embrace a state of life, or to acquire an education or cultural benefits equal to those recognized for men."[5]

Mary Daly's Comment

It is clear that women cannot "embrace a state of life" on the same terms as men, as long as they are excluded from the hierarchy.

The vast theological developments which have taken place in recent years have implications for the specific question of woman's ordination which have not been lost upon progressive theologians. Recognizing the weakness of theological objections, they have openly shifted the whole question to the arenas of sociology and psychology. Thus, in 1966, Father Hans Küng stated: "There are two factors to consider regarding the ordination of women in the Sacred Ministry of the Church. The first is that there are no dogmatic or biblical reasons against it. The second is that there are psychological and sociological factors to be considered. The solution to the problem depends on the sociological conditions of the time and place. It is entirely a matter of cultural circumstances."[6]

41

At least as many men as women within the Catholic church have held that no theological objections exist to ordaining women and that it is a cultural problem, not a theological one. The list includes Fathers Bernard Haring, Jean Daniélou, Georges Tavard, Gregory Baum, Joseph Fichter, Haye van der Meer, and Jose Idigoras. Among the laity there are many, the most outspoken being Dr. Govaart-Halkes, Elizabeth Schussler, Gertrud Heinzelmann, Sydney Callahan, and Mary Daly. The leaders of the small but articulate minority which actively promotes the cause of full ordination of women are theologian Mary Daly in the United States and the lawyer, Gertrud Heinzelmann, of Switzerland.

The most liberal theologians expect the matter of ordination to be decided on the basis of cultural acceptance; yet the response of many to this volatile issue indicates that the climate of opinion is far from receptive. Clerics whose nonsacerdotal functional roles are threatened by professional laymen and laywomen are somewhat defensive about the emergent laity in general and would find it unthinkable to have women colleagues. Women who have raised the issue have suffered *ad hominem* (*ad feminam?*) attacks launched by those who sustain an *idée fixe* concerning clerical forms.[7] In a church which has retained its institutional and liturgical forms for so many centuries, the dramatic transformation that has been effected within a few years has been in general exciting to the young and disquieting to the old. Examples of the dynamic updating of other forms of service to the church lend encouragement to advocates of a female priesthood; yet it is also arguable that this issue is dangerous in that it is divisive and would inevitably divert attention from more basic questions. This last argument could be outdated quickly, of course, should the rate of acceleration of change within the church continue at its present pace for a few years.

Few Catholic theologians, whatever their views on the ordination of women, consider the matter to be urgent; the traditional view is considered to be dominant but not unassailable. It seems very possible, however, that the evolution of the understanding of this question within the Catholic church will follow if not parallel that of the volatile question of birth control. Meanwhile, the matter is officially subsumed under the reevaluation of the role of priest and layman and the pertinence and force of the charismatic revival which claims that from ". . . a theological point of view (and increasingly from psychological and sociological ones, too), the distinction between the sexes is here irrelevant; there are absolutely no dogmatic grounds for opposing preaching by women. Charisms which have been granted to Christians ought to be acknowledged with gratitude and pressed into service." [8] And so the editor of the English edition of *Documents of Vatican II* duly instructs readers that the term "laity" is clearly intended to encompass both sexes.[9]

Many churchmen sympathetic to the desire of Catholic women to participate in ecclesiastical-ministerial functions apparently feel that a way could be found eventually through the revival of a Catholic diaconate, which has been urged by Vatican II and implemented formally by Pope Paul in 1968.[10] The establishment of at least a male diaconate is given urgency by the fact that, as of October 1968, there were 671 counties and 5,000 towns in the United States without a resident priest. The petitions of bishops to establish a male diaconate in Germany, France, Peru, and South Africa have already been granted; more are now pending in Canada and Great Britain. The pattern may become pervasive, particularly since a female diaconate would constitute a revival of the ancient order of deaconess and thereby adhere closely to tradition; for, although women in the early church exercised distinctly ecclesiastical-ministerial roles, they did not perform sacerdotal functions. Be this as it may, it seems clear that any significant changes in the role of women in the Catholic church will accompany basic changes taking place among the laity, particularly with regard to the increased use of professionally trained men and women. As of now, one can cite many examples of minor improvements in the official status of women in the church.

On the other side of the scales there rests the overwhelming respect which unquestionably still is paid the body of tradition that has for so many centuries governed the Catholic church. The one million Roman Catholic nuns who serve the church throughout the world enjoy a professional status which is more definite and secure than that of female church workers in many Protestant denominations and that of deaconesses within the Anglican and the Lutheran churches. Nuns are accorded great esteem, have a sense of professionalism, and hold high positions in the fields of mission work and education and medical work. They have no role beyond that of any lay woman, however, in strictly ecclesiastical functions. The Pauline texts, the Thomistic view of women as subject to men because of intrinsic biological defectiveness and lack of "eminence," the commonly accepted identification of women with the Virgin and an exclusive wife-mother role, and the continuous reiteration of these and similar points by doctors of the church have compelled virtually unanimous respect until quite recently. There has been absolutely no *official* progress on the admission of women to ecclesiastical or liturgical functions. In fact, some of the more ardent advocates of ordination of women have expressed dismay over the results of Vatican II. Previously, in some parts of Europe, women had been serving as acolytes and lectors; the practice has now been banned. It appears to be a case of two steps forward, one backward. In short, the ground-swell of the laity will certainly carry the position of women higher; but the assault on the priesthood will probably be confined to the pages of the avant-garde *National Catholic Reporter* for some time to come.

THE GREEK ORTHODOX CHURCH

The Greek Orthodox Church is looked upon as the most tradition-honoring of the major churches, and a description of the work of the women of the church is a fairly simple task. Their work has been substantial in acts of social service, but since it is seldom regularized or institutionalized it is difficult to weigh. The church has traditionally maintained the view that ". . . institutionalized philanthropy is not love but legalized humanism . . ." and that the true social witness of the church was to be achieved on a personal basis.[11] Orders of nuns minister to social needs, usually on a local basis. A remarkable exception to this rule was experienced during the great famine in Greece in 1941/42. Most men were in the army and the Greek archbishop turned the enormous task of keeping people from starving over to the women of the church. They did a superb job.

Surprisingly, in a formal reply to an invitation to comment upon a WCC Faith and Order study paper on ordination, an Orthodox theologian, J. D. Zizioulas, could say that the study offered ". . . the possibility of a comprehensive ecumenical outlook in which the Orthodox understanding of ordination could take place." And in commenting on the ordination of women he wrote: ". . . Greek theologians could find no theological reasons against such an ordination. Yet the entire matter is so deeply tied up with their tradition that they would find it difficult in their majority to endorse without reservations the rather enthusiastic statements of the paper." [12] An interesting historical note is that deaconesses in the medieval Greek church were ordained until the twelfth century. The ceremony, however, was unlike that accorded a deacon and is described as a "blessing." [13] The Orthodox church and the Eastern churches related to it do not today, however, ordain women. The Mar Thoma Church of Malabar (South India) has been studying the matter through the Scriptures and is, for the time being, withholding a decision.[14]

The Greek church has maintained a school for deaconesses since 1957. Its main purpose is to prepare social workers for positions in church, state, or private secular institutions. Women may study theology, and many do. They are then usually appointed as instructors of religion in schools. They may lecture or preach in halls or schools but not in churches.

NOTES

1. Thomas J. Fleming, "Can the 'Catholic Revolution' Succeed?" *Redbook*, May 1969, p. 77.

2. Michael Novak, "The Underground Church," *Saturday Evening Post*, December 28, 1968/January 11, 1969, p. 67.

3. In the late spring of 1969, a Roman Catholic parish in Edmondton, Alberta, Canada, approved girls for service as "altar boys." The archbishop of the diocese has yet to give the last word. *The Lutheran*, June 4, 1969, p. 45.

4. Mary Daly, *The Church and the Second Sex*, pp. 157-158.

5. *Pastoral Constitution*, part I, chap. 2, n. 29.

6. Daly, *The Church and the Second Sex*, p. 159.

7. Mary Daly, for instance, temporarily lost her teaching post at Boston University, a Catholic institution.

8. Yves Congar, O.P., theological consultant at Vatican II, quoted by Hans Küng, *The Church* (London: Burns and Oates, 1967), p. 378.

9. Walter M. Abbott, ed., *Documents of Vatican II* (New York: Herder and Herder, 1966), p. 500.

10. The decision to establish a permanent diaconate, including married men "of mature years," in the United States was announced by the National Council of Catholic Bishops in 1968.

11. Demetrios J. Constantelos, "Social Consciousness in the Greek Orthodox Church," *Greek Orthodox Theological Review,* vol. 12, no. 3, fall, 1967, p. 320.

12. J. D. Zizioulas, "Some Remarks by an Orthodox on the Study Paper, 'The Meaning of Ordination,'" World Council of Churches Faith and Order Commission, pp. 1, 4.

13. Nicolae Chitescu, "The Ordination of Women: A Comment on the Attitude of the Orthodox Church" in World Council of Churches, *Concerning the Ordination of Women,* p. 60.

14. Elsie Thomas Culver, *Women in the World of Religion,* p. 289.

Chapter 5

In
the Anglican
Communion

The Religious News Service released a story on August 23, 1968, on the Lambeth Conference in London, which had passed a resolution stating that ". . . at present there are no conclusive theological arguments for or against ordination of women to the Anglican priesthood." The RNS then tersely noted that the conference refused to endorse ordination. This episode is typical of the reaction of the Anglican church to what it has called this "most delicate matter" for more than fifty years. Indeed, the anguished debate over the role of women in the church really began when the Anglicans about a century ago revived the institution of the diaconate. Since the Second World War, the matter has been pressed both at the Lambeth Conferences and at official meetings of the bishops, the clergy, and the laity. It must be said, however, that in the course of its long deliberations the church has produced a series of studies several of which rank very high in quality—including the quality of refreshing candor in a literature that is not noted for such.

Actually, one gets a feeling for the mind of the church not from the floor debates but from the calm pages of the reports prepared for the Lambeth Conferences. The Anglican church seems to urge that a solution for its women members should be sought through a new definition of the church's ministry, a reappraisal and renewal of its laity so as to bring the laity in closer communion with the clergy, an upgrading of its diaconate (which in practice is used for men as a preparatory period for the priesthood), and the creation of a concomitant service *short of the priesthood* that would attract the women of the church to a more fruitful use of their gifts. This diaconate would remain a Holy Order, but it would be a lay order. In addition, the church has moved to clarify the status of the deaconess who, through her ordination, dedicates herself to a lifelong service in a Holy Order.

The most recent publications of the Church of England on women and priesthood find theological considerations inconclusive, the word from the Scriptures divided, and the tradition of the church based upon ancient and medieval assumptions about the social role and inferior status of women no longer acceptable. The church is invited to take

---

**A SAMPLE OF ANGLICAN FEELING FROM
THE LAMBETH CONFERENCE OF 1968**

In some provinces there is a strong case for women being ordained to the priesthood; in others this would not yet be consonant with the character of the culture in which the Church is at work. . . . The ministry in the world, to the world, and for the world demands that the Church corporately, and Christians individually and in groups, face the problem of the right use of the resources which God has placed at man's disposal. How are these resources to be used responsibly and creatively? The Church must be rich in the resources of grace and wise in the use of human and material resources for her ministry. The Church must be poor in avoiding dependence upon or seeking after riches and resources for herself or of Christian groups and individuals.[1]

"fresh initiatives" by leaders who frequently refer to the gradual acceptance by other churches of a full ministry exercised by an ordained woman. As of now it is obvious that many of the bishops of the Church of England and many laymen consider it to be the major obligation of the church to educate its people to think constructively on the matter. It is the clergy who are holding back. One may be quickly instructed by examining the votes in the church assembly.

The picture presented by the distaff side of the laity, in terms of recognized service to the church, is dismal. Out of 14,000 parishes in the Church of England, fewer than 500 have women on their staffs. Of all the women employed full-time in church vocations, 1,500 are members of religious communities, 460 are welfare workers, 450 are parish workers, 260 are Church Army sisters, 65 are deaconesses. In summary, as of now, the church does not know what to do with able, intelligent, and educated women.

To see the laity in a new light is to see the role of women in a new light. The lengthy and sober contemplations of the church on this subject often move on to include the priesthood, and often end on a very sour note:

> There is . . . an increasing number of able, educated women who, while not demanding for themselves admission to the ordained priesthood, believe that there should be no obstacles in the way of a woman who feels called to that priesthood. The reason so few women are demanding entry to the priesthood may be that until recently such a possibility was not considered practicable. Powerful arguments have been raised against permitting women to become priests: the very term "woman priest" suggests an impossibility. But in the mid-20th century many sacred conceptions and holy institutions are being revised and refashioned. Then too there is the influence of the practical: the day of the woman priest may yet come on the ground that not enough men are taking up the calling.[2]

The noted Anglican bishop, John A. T. Robinson, after having met Margit Sählin, the priest-theologian of the Lutheran Church of Sweden, said: "If anyone asks me in the future whether I believe in women priests, I can only say that I have seen one. And by any test known to the Gospel I find myself unable to deny the grace of orders or to resist the Holy Spirit."[3] It may well be that the dangers to their ecumenical fellowship frequently underscored both by Swedish Lutherans and Anglicans have been exaggerated.[4]

It comes again as an expression of the ambivalence of the Anglicans' careful course between caution and daring that at the 1968 Lambeth Conference the bishops voted to recommend as an interim step that Anglican churches be encouraged to allow duly qualified women to share in the conduct of worship, to preach, baptize, read the Scripture at Holy Communion, and assist in the distribution of the sacramental elements. These decisions and recommendations are not binding on the church, although Lambeth statements historically have had considerable influence. In any case, Dr. Kathleen Bliss, until recently general secretary of the Church of England Board of Education, preached a sermon not long ago in the university church of St. Mary the Great in Cambridge. Dr. Bliss, fifty-eight years old and the mother of three daughters, is now a lecturer in religious studies at Sussex University and acts as secretary for the Council on Women in the Church's Ministry.

Only one woman has ever been ordained by the Anglican church. She was Miss Li Tim Oi, of the church in China, and her ordination seemed to be required because of drastic need for her services during World War II. "This ordination . . . was later 'deplored' by the Lambeth Conference as 'a most unwelcome unilateral act,' and she was asked not to take advantage of it."[5]

The Anglican Church of Canada and the Episcopal Church (United States) have produced lively elements who are in favor not only of a much broader service in the church for lay women, both professional and nonprofessional, but also the ordination of women as priests. The Canadian church is more prone to take action than its American neighbor in the Anglican communion. In 1968, its House of Bishops, acting on the Lambeth Conference vote of 1968, granted permission to "lay persons, either men or women," to administer the wine and bread at Holy Communion—the first such action taken by any body within the Anglican church. This action, significantly enough, was taken to "restore the proper place and function of the lay members of the Church." [6] The Canadian church, currently considering merger with the United Church of Canada, is also debating the matter of recognizing fifty ordained women pastors of the latter body, which has made this action a stipulation of the merger. And the Anglican bishop Carman J. Queen of St. Clair, suffragan of the Huron diocese, upon his return from the 1968 Lambeth Conference announced that the Canadian church will proceed to discuss the ordination of women as deaconesses and priests. [7]

On the other side of the ledger is the disposition to let well enough alone. Women delegates to an Anglican diocesan session recently voted against allowing women to be church wardens. It would be ". . . a great disservice to males to strip them of that office. . . ." [8] Whether the women would take similar action on other offices is a question. The real point is that the Anglican Church of Canada seems likely to conduct its discussions with greater alacrity and take action with greater freedom than its English or its American sister churches.

In the Episcopal Church (United States), the woman problem seems to be surfacing in tow of the civil rights crisis, the black revolution, the students' revolt, and the now burgeoning women's liberation movement. The controversies whirling about the late Bishop James Pike seemed somehow to set things off. For instance, in 1965 he ordained Sister Phyllis Edwards to the position of "perpetual deacon," a position that ranks as clergy. For this action he was reprimanded by the church but not excommunicated. Bishop Pike drew attention to the parallel between the position of women in the church and elsewhere and the position of the Negro, a parallel first established by Gunnar Myrdahl in his book, *The American Dilemma.* Other flashes began to appear. A woman, Mrs. Harold C. Kelleran, professor of pastoral theology at the Episcopal Theological Seminary in Alexandria, Virginia, was appointed to a committee, chaired by Nathan Pusey, president of Harvard University, to study theological education. In 1967, the House of Deputies finally approved by a large majority the seating of female delegates—the last of the Protestant churches to do so with the single exception of the Lutheran Church—Missouri Synod. The House of Bishops also approved. Since two successive triennial conventions must also approve the action, it will, however, be 1973 before women delegates may attend the ruling assembly of the church.

Something of great importance is happening within the church. It is evident in the confrontation at South Bend, Indiana, in August, 1969, when at their regular triennial convention the House of Bishops (200 of them) and the House of Deputies (696 clergymen and laymen) laid aside their normal procedures and invited to plenary sessions 234 extra representatives, 78 blacks, 78 youths, and 78 women, to help frame legislative recommendations. Among the rank and file of lay women there is a growing disposition to leave the Christmas bazaars and the overstaffed altar guilds to get on with the work of the church *together* with the men. After voting in 1967 to raise $2.25 million to help the church meet the urban crisis, the women began to question the usefulness of separate units. The Episcopal Church Women of West Texas have eliminated their board, holding that "to preserve our present organization would be to deny [our] unity and continue the hindrances to mission and service which we believe are perpetuated by our divisions." [9] The women are supporting experiments that include team ministries, full use of professionally trained workers, ordained or unordained, the relaxing of prohibitions against women in local vestries and in diocesan conventions, and lay involvement regardless of sex at every level of decision-making. Several dioceses have experimented with launching cooperative or "meshed" projects. This quiet pressure for partnership may pave the way for a renaissance among the Anglican laity. A very sensitive point touched upon again and again in the literature of the Anglican church is that the bishops and the clergy, looked upon for so long as the pillars of the Anglican church, have become so clericalized that the consequent isolation of the clergy from one another and from the laity has become a source of great weakness.

One cannot escape the impression that the Anglican church, moving cautiously and fully aware of the possible danger to ecumenism in its words and actions, is yet moving firmly in the direction of greater participation of all lay people, including women. It is sharply aware of its need for professionally trained assistants. The Council on Women in the Church's Ministry, the Society for the Equal Ministry of Men and Women of the Church, and St. Joan's

International Alliance, and their Canadian and American sympathizers, may be making more progress in the face of drastic needs of the Anglican communion than it has been possible to document. The needs may succeed in freeing the frozen assets of the churches and, at long last, outweigh the fears—ecumenical or other.

NOTES

1. From the Lambeth Conference (1968), *Reports of Sections,* II: "The Renewal of the Church in Ministry," pp. 1-2.

2. Cecil Northcott, "Women Priests in England?" *Christian Century,* January 24, 1968, pp. 101-102.

3. Cecil Northcott, "Woolwich's Resolution," *Christian Century,* May 20, 1964, p. 328.

4. Some observers of the ecumenical scene, including Peter Day, the ecumenical officer of the Episcopal Church (United States), were discouraged when, in the summer of 1969, the Anglican Convocation of Canterbury and York turned down reunion with the Methodist Church of Great Britain. With 75 percent of each church's total vote required, the Anglicans produced only 69 percent. The Archbishop of Canterbury, however, is optimistic and ready for another try: "... there is no cause for despair," he said.

5. Culver, *Women in the World of Religion,* p. 289.

6. *New York Times,* October 25, 1968.

7. Ibid.

8. *Tempo,* August 1, 1969, p. 4.

9. Ibid., p. 11.

Chapter 6

In Major
Churches Here
and Abroad

THE UNITED PRESBYTERIAN CHURCH IN THE U.S.A.

Presbyterians in the United States have been studying
the problem of the ordination of women since 1953. As
early as 1955 what was called an "overture" on ordination
was approved by the general assembly and sent to the
presbyteries. Three years later the main branch of the
church wrote it into its constitution, with the Southern
Presbyterians following in 1964. Meanwhile, in 1958 the
merger of the two churches into the United Presbyterian
Church in the United States of America, hastened or perhaps even necessitated a thoroughgoing study of the whole
ministry of the church which finally, after four years, came
out as a collection of materials for discussion throughout
the church under the title *The Church and Its Changing
Ministry*.[1] Very little of that study related to the role of
women has been utilized until recently, in spite of the fact
that Presbyterians have been ordaining women since 1956.
And none of it received the publicity the Church of Scotland received when, on May 22, 1968, after a campaign of
almost forty years, the general assembly voted to consider
women as eligible for ordination on equal terms with men.
Ten deaconesses were immediately identified as being eligible, and indeed one of them was ordained by the Presbytery of Aberdeen one year later. Still another has been

licensed as a probationer to the ministry—the first step toward ordination in the Church of Scotland—and six women have since directed appeals for ordination to the general assembly of the church.

The Calvinist church tradition allows more elbow room than some others in that there are *four* offices—pastor, teacher, elder, and deacon—that might provide doors of entry for qualified women to serve the church. At this point the difficulties mount: the European Calvinist churches insist that only the pastoral ministry is "bestowed and sanctioned" by ordination. The United Presbyterian Church ordains deacons and elders as well. Few churches now claim that there are clear theological and biblical reasons for the exclusion of women from certain offices and tasks of the church; they must then, perforce, approach the problem of ordination from the standpoint of tradition. The confusion on this matter the Calvinist churches share with many others.

ORDINATION, CONFUSION, AND DIVERSIFIED MINISTRIES

With regard to the elder and the deacon, their ministries must indeed be church functions. They are nonetheless considered as of another nature than the pastoral ministry. This became clear from the moment we first spoke of the "laity" and the "clergy" in our churches. The elder and the deacon were then considered "laymen" and the pastor a "clergyman." More than one of our church constitutions uses the term "clergy" to designate the body of pastors.

At present, under the pressure of necessity, but we believe also under the impulse of the Spirit, increasing numbers of our Churches are beginning to recognize and to institute other church ministries. On the one hand, new needs have appeared, and on the other, men and women have heard the call of God to dedicate their entire lives to the service of the Church in order to exercise a ministry different from, but complementary to, the pastoral ministry. . . .

It is necessary at this point to state precisely why the Churches restrict the administration of the sacraments to the pastors, because it is this fact more than any other that makes acceptable to so many people the erroneous idea that the pastorate is a sort of priesthood. This restriction is a matter of order, not a sacramental matter. It is in order that it will be clear that there occurs in the administration of the sacrament an act of the Church; so that no one ought to perform it without the mandate of the Church. The evidence that this is so is provided by the regular practice among pastors of granting to the unordained the right, among others, to administer the sacraments.

But what then is ordination for the Reformed Churches? As strange as it seems, they have never declared this with precision. While the Catholic Churches have formulated in a clear and coherent doctrine the sense and the import of their ordinations, we find nothing similar on ordination in our confessions of faith or our liturgies. The Second Helvetic Confession of Faith, for example, says simply: "Those chosen by the lawful election of the Church shall be put in possession of the ministry by the elders with public prayers and the laying on of hands. . . ."

If this is the meaning and import of ordination, and if the pastoral ministry, although different from the other ministries of the Church, is nevertheless of the same nature, does it not follow that all those whom God calls to a ministry of the Church that requires their full effort and time should be ordained to it in the same manner?

There should be for each ministry of the Church a corresponding ordination proper to it. When the day comes that our Churches really recognize, with all that this implies, a plurality of church ministries, and ordain to their respective ministries all those who in response to the summons of God wish to dedicate their lives, an end will be put to the confusion that now reigns in this matter. . . .

The problem of the church ministry of women, neglected for so long, is at present a preoccupation of Churches across the entire world, a subject that they are investigating thoroughly. It cannot be said that a full solution has yet been proposed. But it is permissible to wonder if at the moment, when at last the Churches have grasped the urgency of the matter, they have posed the question in the most correct terms. One is often limited to vindicating the right of women to undertake tasks hitherto reserved exclusively for the man rather than seeking those for which the woman's own nature more particularly qualifies her. . . .

If the pastorate had not been regarded for so long in our Churches as the only true church ministry; if it had not been the only one sanctioned by an ordination; would we have sought the solution of the problem of the church ministry of women in the pastoral office?[2]

The favorable treatment women have received in the Presbyterian churches generally is closely linked with the high status the laity in general enjoys. Although it was possible for a Mr. See to be tried in 1877 by the New York presbytery for allowing two women to speak in his church, the Presbyterians were the *first* of the major denominations in the United States to give full ordination rights to women. For a good many years now the Presbyterians have welcomed women to the boards, committees, and commissions of the church at all levels, and since 1930 the church has ordained women as deacons and elders, and by virtue of these offices permitted them to administer communion.[3]

In June 1967, the United Presbyterian Church assembly voted a three-year study specifically on the status of women with the recommendation that the task force become a standing committee. Two years later this authorization was renewed and the permanent committee was set up with the Reverend Priscilla Chaplin as chairman. In assuming her duties, she made clear how even in the progressive

Presbyterian church a whole complex of behavior patterns had developed which had relegated women to an inferior status. Although women constituted almost 60 percent of the laity, only a few more than 15 percent of all ordained elders and 40 percent of all ordained deacons were women. The percentage of women ministers was 0.518. Five ordained women are working for the church in New England, but not one is working in a parish. Uneasy about the failure of its progressive stance to yield better results, the Reverend Diane Dennis called for a conference of women to meet "without agenda, without male interference, and without the label of United Presbyterian Women's sponsorship." "If you have millions for blacks, as you should," she said, "give us a couple of bucks to worry about women." [4]

THE UNITED METHODIST CHURCH

The World Methodist Council, in a valiant attempt to describe its structures, figures that, aside from the mother church in England (which has just been denied merger with the Anglican church) with its six overseas regions, and the United Methodist Church with twenty-seven regional communions in unity with it, there are twenty-one autonomous Methodist churches not yet formally affiliated with the World Methodist Council.

This complicated organism, with its necessarily heavy emphasis upon local flexibility, certainly has obvious advantages in terms of providing a wide range of opportunities to serve and to experiment in Christian service. In the eyes of the officials of the church the *disadvantages* of the structure which relate most closely to our subject derive from the condition that women's work has been concentrated with such a singular intensity upon local situations and miscellaneous good works that the church has been deprived of their leadership in a broader area. The stereotype syndrome—a chronic complaint of the woman church worker —seems especially severe to the Methodists who, in spite of their relative freedom from theological restraints and ecclesiastical traditions, fall heir to the same conditions that afflict other denominations. Ronald A. Witmer, assistant pastor at the Park Avenue Methodist Church of New York City, addresses himself to these familiar questions: Why are Protestant women's groups largely ineffective? Why is leadership in most local churches predominantly male? Why are stereotypes of church women so abundant? Why is leadership so hard to find? ". . . All over small-town and suburban America, the unhappiness which has no name, the frustration and boredom felt by many intelligent women with much to give but no place to give it, has been an important, tragic factor in family life." "Church leaders have retarded the freedom of women by insisting that they remain by themselves, segregated from the men, bent almost exclusively upon home, church dinners and miscellaneous good works." He chides the church men for being reluctant to yield authority and women for meekly accepting their assigned roles.[5] Methodist lay women as well as pastors' wives are now being called upon to work with their husbands to develop new congregations, to do pastoral calling, and to work out church projects under the New Church Development plan.[6]

The church reports that there has been a modest but steady increase in the number of Methodist women ordained, i.e., *"under appointment with pastoral office,"* from 246 in 1964 to 278 in 1968.[7] The single restriction laid upon ordained women prior to 1956 was that they had to be assigned under local provision and not under the itinerant rule. Since 1956, however, women ministers as well as men follow the direction of the bishops in their assignment.[8] One of the most amazing of them, the Reverend Margaret Henricksen, who served as pastor to *seven* congregations in northern Maine, in 1969 became the first woman to be appointed as superintendent of a district of the United Methodist Church—in Bangor, Maine.[9] Her book *Seven Steeples* gives a graphic description of her pastoral experience.[10]

It is interesting to note that the Methodists of the United States, who ordained and called into service the first female theologian in the country a hundred years ago, and who also produced the first woman member of a theological faculty, at Newbury Seminary, Vermont, in 1837, is just now, in the fall of 1969, planning to launch a formal study of the "woman problem."

Methodists are as varied in their world picture as they are in the United States. In South America Methodist women have had the same rights as men since 1960. In England and Australia they may not be ordained, but in England the deaconesses may serve the sacraments and sit on examining committees. Irish Methodists have "fully ordained" women ministers, and Korea, New Zealand, and South Africa have no bars against ordination. In Sarawak the president of a Methodist theological seminary is a woman, Dr. Ivy Chow, and in North Sumatra Chinese District, the Reverend Gusta Robinett is district superintendent of the church.[11]

THE AMERICAN BAPTIST CONVENTION

The Baptist churches of the United States have never restricted ordination to the male sex, but most of its women pastors are concentrated, as in the past, in New England. In May 1967, the American Baptist Convention moved to undertake a study of new ways to undergird structures for its professional ministry, and it was made very clear that such structures were intended to serve both men and women pastors. Placement services, adequate compensation, continuing education, and assistance for professional development and all related concerns were to be concentrated in a Regional Center for the Ministry.[12] There are, however, no provisions in the plan for the *recruitment* of women, professionally trained or otherwise, for staff assistants or for pastorates. In August 1969, Dr. Culbert G. Rutenber, president of the American Baptist Convention, urged the women of his church to push harder to win their goals.[13]

THE UNITED CHURCH OF CHRIST

The United Church of Christ (formed by a union of two already-merged denominations, the General Council of the Congregational Christian Churches and the Evangelical and Reformed Church) does ordain women, as do other churches who follow the Congregational tradition. Its fellow Congregational Church of England and Wales has ordained eighty women in fifty-one years, and "is not sorry," according to its observer at the Lambeth Conference of 1968. It was this representative who raised at the conference the age-old question, "Is God masculine?"[14]

The United Church of Christ made a large contribution to a developing pattern of combining men's and women's work units by forming a department of the laity—the first of the larger denominations to do so.

THE CHURCH OF THE BRETHREN

The Church of the Brethren has ordained women since 1960, although the church historically has never had a "doctrine" of ordination. Its tradition since the time of the

63

Reformation has been one of consistent and radical protest against "institutionalist sacerdotalism." [15] Yet it admits having absorbed concepts of ordination from the churches around it. The proper ceremony is the laying on of hands used in baptism, in healing, in the commissioning of workers who represent the church in its worldwide programs of missions, relief, and rehabilitation, as well as in the calling of ministers. The theologian who thus interpreted the Church of the Brethren view noted that although he was "ordained" to the ministry before he married, the wedding ceremony included a laying on of hands to symbolize his wife's desire to join him in Christian service.

It is of interest that a church so radically firm in its position should have been influenced by a practice and adopted a vocabulary that is antipathetic to its tradition, and that the functional view of the office of the "ordained" minister should include his wife. The seat of authority for all such ordaining, commissioning, or laying on of hands is the *gemeinde,* the congregation.

"The crucial question," this interpreter says, "is whether the New Testament evidence similarly does not point toward such a flexible, broad-focused, *gemeinde*-centered practice." The *gemeinde* determines who is qualified as teacher, preacher, finance secretary, or janitor, and just when the laying on of hands is meaningful and appropriate. This practice would leave the congregation or church body theoretically free to decide whether maleness or femaleness is an advantage or disadvantage functionally in the performance of a given task.

THE CHURCHES OF SWITZERLAND

In Switzerland the debate over the role of women in the churches has been closely tied in with three factors: the rising demand that women be allowed to vote along with male citizens, the catastrophic shortage of pastors, and the heavy influence of the churches of predominately Catholic cantons. Incidentally, it comes as a great surprise to most people who have long looked upon Switzerland as one of the most democratic countries in the world that

ORDINATION OF WOMEN IN SWITZERLAND

. . . the ordination of women today [1966] is extended without any discussion in most churches of German Switzerland. There is only one service of ordination for men and women. The terrible shortage of pastors has profoundly affected the whole situation. In Zürich a curious thing happened which is worth mentioning. After the decision to ordain women was made, all theologically trained women were called together and ordained at once, no matter whether they were married or unmarried, whether they had ever worked as a *Pastorin* or not!

In some cantons of Switzerland *Pastorinnen* are eligible for a pastorate without any restrictions. In others they are only eligible in parishes which have more than one pastor.

In French Switzerland the catholicising movement "*Eglise et Liturgie*" has been of great influence and has created considerable difficulties for women's work in the church. This is especially true for the canton of Waadt. This development indicates that any stronger emphasis on the exercise of "priestly" functions automatically excludes women, or at least reduces the scope of their services.

In the Roman Catholic church we are rather backward in Switzerland. I am not even sure whether women can study theology and work for their D.D. On the other hand, the divinity courses for women *(Frauen-Theologiekurse)* in the Catholic church are well attended. Through these courses women attain the right to give religious instruction even in the upper classes of high schools.[16]

in many of its cantons women have never had the vote and that many women do not want the vote. Nonetheless, Switzerland may provide one more example of a situation where rather rigid conservatism, when it *does* begin to yield, does so with great rapidity. During the last decade the churches of one canton after another have decided to declare women eligible for service in a congregation. In 1967 there were seventy-five theologians working in the church. A year later seventy-seven women were studying theology in Swiss universities, and in January 1969, Swiss theological students, both men and women, called for a "1969 Reformation" starting with new concepts of ministry which would make full use of team ministries, including nontheologians, and new experiments in forms of worship. It is expected that more and more women will be actively recruited for service in the church within a very short time.

THE CHURCHES OF FRANCE

Since France, of course, is predominately Roman Catholic, French women who work for the church or seek a larger role in its work are under the same handicaps as other Roman Catholic women all over the world.

French Lutherans, however, have ordained women, but a woman must give up her parish if she marries, except in Strasbourg, where she is allowed to resume her ministry when she is widowed or divorced.[17]

What is happening in the Waldensian church of France, the oldest "protestant" church in Christendom, illustrates that the wave of the future is washing over a wide area. The Waldensian church was established in the twelfth century on the principles of individual responsibility for interpreting Scripture and the necessity to make the Bible available to all people in their own language. This church, now numbering about thirteen thousand members, was influential in the thinking of the great reformers Wycliffe and Huss. In 1962 the church voted to accept the practice of the ordination of women and provided that women may be elected to any ecclesiastical position including the highest office, that of moderator. On August 20, 1967, two women were ordained.

OTHER CHURCHES IN EUROPE

"Czechoslovakia and Denmark were ordaining women in 1958, but only in 1964 did the clergy association of the Lutheran Church of Norway admit a woman to membership. . . . A woman ordained in Norway does not conduct marriages or funerals. . . . The Evangelical Lutheran Church of the Netherlands has given women full ordination rights since 1929. The Slovak Lutheran Church has for years ordained women as assistants to male pastors. They have now ordained a woman to full charge of a bilingual (Slovak and Magyar) church. Austria makes a nice distinction: they voted in 1956 'on theological grounds' that women have equal *worth* but not equal *nature!* They demonstrated what they meant by putting women *theologians* on an equal financial footing with pastors." [18]

THE CHURCH OF INDIA

The religious heritage of modern Indian women is nothing short of fantastic. In spite of the magnificent efforts of religious reformers from the twelfth century on, the plight of Indian women has been closely associated with a collection of taboos deeply ingrained in the rich culture of that land. A poignant and sympathetic account for the general reader is given in Elsie Thomas Culver's book, *Women in the World of Religion,* which has provided many insights for all who work in this field. "The fear of taboo," she writes, "has a stronger hold on men's minds than most of us are ever willing to admit, and it is never more firmly entrenched than when it has laid its cuckoo eggs in the nest of religion." [19] She tells of the notable battle waged by twelve women members of the Indian parliament in support of the Hindu Code Bill prescribing basic human rights for women, and particularly their attack upon the commonly-heard opposing argument: "Our traditional religion must be upheld."

When the British took over the rule of India they consulted the Brahman priests on civil and religious affairs; the Brahmans took advantage of the opportunity to perpetuate and extend their caste prejudices. As Mrs. Renuka Ray, one of the twelve women mentioned above, put it: " 'Consequently, the British pressed down upon the people of India harsh and ridiculously cruel laws, believing these were historical customs in the land. The worst to suffer were the women.' " Mrs. Ray is quoted further as saying that the Hindu Code Bill " '. . . does nothing but restore to women the rights they held in ancient times, but which were taken away from them by the priests and the British.' " [20]

This heritage, both civil and religious, spells out both tragedy and opportunity for the Christian Indian woman. She sees a woman leading the state, she sees women in the parliament, education is now available to a considerable number of her sex, the society is in such a state of flux that new opportunities seem to be opening on every hand. Yet the large reservoir of talent available to society and to the church remains untapped because the cultural traditions that bind women within Indian society at large continue to keep her "in her place" within the church.

Along with other clergymen of India, Lutheran pastors are unwilling, on the whole, to promote change. Women sit in considerable numbers on decision-making bodies such as the Federation of Evangelical Lutheran Churches in India and the National Christian Council, and they participate in synod and general church conventions. But in all posts their remuneration is much lower, their job security practically nonexistent, and their status and prestige low regardless of their competence. Indian women have replaced foreign missionary women in every service of the church— as teachers and directors of the Bible training programs for women, as heads of educational institutions, as directors of social-mission institutions for the handicapped, and as superintendents of nurses and nursing schools and as medical superintendents of hospitals. But the church sets their salaries, and because the salaries are so low the problem of the recruitment of professionally trained women is becoming acute. When a plan was conceived to set up a deaconess-type community that would help compensate for the low salaries of Indian church women, there was interest among the women but little support was forthcoming from the pastors.[21]

It is a foregone conclusion that professional services rendered to Indian society by Christian institutions largely powered by women of the church will now "go secular." And this may be a good thing. But the Christian church everywhere must be prepared to face the charge that the church does not really sustain its claim that its way is the way of freedom, of wholeness, and of healing.

NOTES

1. Robert Clyde Johnson, ed., *The Church and Its Changing Ministry* (Philadelphia: Office of the General Assembly, The United Presbyterian Church in the United States of America, 1961).

69

2. Henri d'Espine, "Ordination and the Diversified Ministries of the Church," in Johnson, ed., *The Church and Its Changing Ministry,* pp. 118-123. Henri d'Espine is professor of Theology at the University of Geneva.

3. Culver, *Women in the World of Religion,* p. 216.

4. *Presbyterian Life,* June 15, 1969, p. 36.

5. Ronald A. Witmer, "Women in the Church," *The Methodist Woman,* October 1968, pp. 28-29.

6. Ralph T. Mirse, "Women in the New Church Development," *Response,* May 1969.

7. In 1963 there were 380 ordained women in the United Methodist Church (Culver, *Women in the World of Religion,* p. 290). Obviously, one-third of the women theologians of the church were not in office.

8. This information was taken from the yearbooks of the Methodist church.

9. Natalie Hantsmeyer, "Indomitable Spirit," *The Methodist Woman,* December 1967, p. 20.

10. Margaret Henricksen, *Seven Steeples* (New York: Harper and Row, Harper Chapel Books, 1967).

11. Culver, *Women in the World of Religion,* pp. 290-291.

12. *Pastor,* May 1967, pp. 1-5.

13. *Tempo,* August 1, 1969, p. 4.

14. Dr. John Huxtable, secretary of the Congregational Church of England and Wales.

15. Vernard Eller, "A Church of the Brethren Response to the Study Paper, 'The Meaning of Ordination,'" World Council of Churches Faith and Order Commission, p. 1.

16. Marga Bührig, "Position of Women in the Church," pp. 282-289.

17. Culver, *Women in the World of Religion,* p. 290.

18. Ibid.

19. Ibid., p. 249.

20. Ibid., p. 250.

21. The information in this paragraph was communicated to the commission by a missionary in India.

Chapter 7

In the
Lutheran Church
of Germany

Lutheran churches abroad are finally allowing women to work within the fold in any capacity for which they are academically and personally qualified—yea, even unto ordination! Moreover, the crises within all the churches are so severe that the particular problem of the ordination of women may well seem a minor threat even to the most conservative churchman.[1] The German situation is particularly important because it was basically shaped by a society in crisis—during and after World War II, when extreme pressures reduced the problem of the role of women in the work of the church to its essentials. It was on this level that the most liberal and most conservative theologians and clergy of the German church did battle.

As the pressures in our own society mount, we look with more and more understanding to the German experiences of the last thirty-five years. Within this period the German churches, both Catholic and Protestant, were forced to face at once the totalitarian dogmas of National Socialism and Communism and the pseudoreligions of race, state, and ideology. These years saw the closing of seminaries, the intense secularization of society, and the visible disintegration of the traditional parish-congregation concept of church organization. Then, after the war, and just as signs of new vitality among the laity and, indeed, a new surge of religious interest were demonstrated by, for instance, the

71

reaction to the *Kirchentag* celebrations and the growth of German varieties of the underground church, the church was again threatened by the separation of church and state and the loss of financial support by the state. East Germany and West Germany have provided Christendom with a pre-run on problems that are certain to plague the churches of many denominations in the years to come.

The reactions of the German church to its traumatic experiences have been pragmatic: women professionally trained in theology have been ordained in considerable numbers in both East and West Germany under a variety of state and church laws. The hierarchy has been on the whole liberal and the congregations remarkably responsive. The latest statistics available indicate that there are about six hundred women theologians in East and West Germany, about four hundred of whom are actively involved in carrying on the duties of a pastor.

This is not to say, however, that there has not been controversy. The very lively postwar debate largely evaporated after twenty-five of the twenty-six regional Protestant churches voted to provide for the ordination and service of women theologians. The one exception was the 2.6 million-member Lutheran Church of Bavaria, where the population is 70 percent Catholic. Most of the *Landeskirchen* (the state churches of each of the political units in the Federal Republic) want and appreciate these services and have made a real effort to use them appropriately. But in 1968 the whole controversy was reactivated when the ordination of women became a point of theological debate between the "Confessionalists" (*Bekenntnisbewegung,* a combination of pietistic, orthodox, and conservative theologians) and the liberal theologians. The Confessionalists' point of view was that the admission of women to the ministry must be seen as a symptom of the inner disintegration and secularization of the church. These laws, they said, were an alarming sign of the necessity for repentance on the part of Lutheran congregations and their pastors, who should, according to Acts 5:29, be confessing their obedience to God rather than men. The Confessionalists wish not only to stop the practice of ordaining women but also to forbid their studying theology. This rather bumptious movement, however, has little of the revolutionary élan or the enthusiasm and bright spirit that characterizes its major competitors—the followers of the "new theology" who attack the church establishment and wish to witness to the faith outside the church. In any event, to that part of the general public still interested in the church, the whole controversy seems irrelevant.

For two decades women pastors have been well received by most church officials and by their own colleagues. The restrictions laid upon them are gradually being removed. In 1965 the most conservative churches in eastern Saxony and Mecklenburg voted to ordain women to a full ministry in the church, except that they were not permitted to preside at weddings and funerals. Recently, the Church of Hannover removed two restrictions: that a woman minister must serve in a large urban congregation where a male pastor would be the "first among equals," and that she must resign as *Pastorin* after marriage.[2] Three other conditions work toward a fuller use of women in the church: the necessity for the churches to get more and more involved in secular life, with an accompanying increase in opportunities for professionally educated women; the coming separation of church and state, which will remove the security long enjoyed by the clergy; and the drastic shortage in pastors—so drastic, indeed (there are currently about seventeen hundred vacancies in the German churches), that the Church of Hannover, one of the most flexible of the

Landeskirchen, has taken action to make it possible for a lay Christian to become a pastor without theological studies after ten years of full-time service to the church.

One of the implications here seems to be that women, who have traditionally been used in all Western societies as a reserve labor force, will be more willing than their male colleagues to face financial insecurity when state churches "go private." At present state churches, along with religious education in the public schools, are still supported by taxes which a citizen automatically pays unless he specifically asks to be absolved. Many Germans do not make this request even though they do not attend church services or work in the church because they make use of the services of the church in the traditional ceremonies of baptism, confirmation, marriage, and burial. The German churches thus face a dual burden: they must devise a variety of new ministries to serve an increasingly secular society; and they will soon lose the financial support of the state. The radical readjustments that will have to be made will tax the ingenuity and human resources of the churches to the utmost, and some German churchmen look for guidance to patterns of service and support that have been developed in the United States. The one advantage these churches now possess over their sister churches in America is their freedom to make full use of their backlog of educated female talent.[3]

According to one woman pastor who is a close observer of these trends, a certain "demythologization" of the pastoral office has taken place. Whether this development is due to the secularization of society or to the modest increase in female pastors is a moot question, but apparently the laity and a majority of the clergy find it easy to accept. This *Pastorin* feels that the general attitude is best portrayed in a book, *Women in the Pulpit,* written by a prominent German churchman, Dr. Richard von Weizsäcker, president of the German Evangelical *Kirchentag*. He writes:

> I assume that it is really only a question of time until we shall have passed the period of discussions about *Theologin-nengesetze* [laws pertaining to women theologians]. I believe we will have to come to the common recognition that not the woman, but rather the immature [*Unmündige*], has to be silent in the congregation, no matter what sex, and that neither man nor woman in the ministry asks for theoretical but rather for practical differentiations. . . . We shall have to examine the gifts of the individual, be it male or female, layman or theologian, close to the core of the congregation or more on the periphery. From now on we shall have to distribute the tasks in order to meet the challenges of our time—challenges which confront us in the light of the gospel.[4]

In view of the "backlog" of female professional theologians and church workers, in view of the need, and in view of the general approval of the higher officials of the churches and most of their colleagues, it must nevertheless be admitted that church boards on the whole have been slow in sending women into vacant parishes. In 1966 alone, 659 of 13,748 vacancies could not be filled for lack of pastors. But there were 252 women (*Pastorinnen*) candidates available for the 159 places "planned" to be allotted to women pastors. No official explanation of this situation was available. How the stewardship of talent shall be exercised is not, and perhaps never can be, clear. Still, the number of women who are studying theology is steadily increasing, and even if one takes into consideration that more than half of these students will discontinue formal study because of marriage, the number of practicing *Pastorinnen* will doubtless grow. Women constituted 16 percent of all theological students in Germany in the year 1963/64.

The paradoxes and complications on the German scene

are compounded by the great variations in official church practices with regard to ordination, preaching, and the administration of the sacraments, the independent leadership of a congregation, and views as to the marital state of the *Pastorin*. As frustrating and vexatious as this situation is for the *Pastorinnen* as well as the church officials, it does not necessarily reflect recalcitrance, obstructive tactics, or bad spirit. Doubtless it results from a combination of these factors, plus some problems that stem from the women themselves. It may simply reflect the pain of transition. In any event, a somewhat detailed review of these complications would be instructive for churches everywhere.

First problem: ordination. The most progressive and one of the latest laws to be promulgated is that of the Lutheran Church of Oldenburg, whose bishop is Hans-Heinrich Harms. Ordination is not explicitly mentioned in the law but is assumed in that it provides identical rules for men and for women. In the Lutheran Church of Hannover (Bishop Lilje), ordination for women is expressly mentioned in a law passed in 1963. However, a liturgical commission was asked specifically to work out an ordination ceremony for women. Apparently the formula for men must not be used!

The Lutheran Church of Schleswig-Holstein attempted to solve the problem by a two-pronged approach in the law. It speaks of *Pastorinnen* who are ordained and of *Kirchenratinnen* (church counselors) who are not ordained. Both have the same training and both are admitted to preaching and to the administration of the sacraments. The only difference is the matter of marriage, which must have been the reason for this twofold law. If a *Pastorin* marries she must give up her place, but a *Kirchenratin* who marries may continue in her work.

This explicit relating of ordination and celibacy discloses a basic misunderstanding of the office. It is strange that this point is significant only if women are concerned. Apparently it has nothing to do with the idea that a wife shall stay at home and raise children. After all, the *Kirchenratin*—with almost the same rights—can work. It is said again and again that ordination is something for the whole life and not only for a certain period of time. There seems to be no substantial theological argument for this attitude; it can, however, be understood as a direct inheritance from the Catholic concept of priesthood which includes the idea of an "indelible character." This twofold law is very imprecise and most unsatisfactory for all concerned. It creates difficulties and tensions between a *clerus major* and *clerus minor* (*Pastorin* and *Kirchenratin*) who have exactly the same academic background and are attempting to cooperate in the same parish—a situation which asks for trouble.

Second problem: preaching and the administration of the sacrament. All *Landeskirchen* that ordain women automatically allow them to preach and to administer the sacraments. But some explicitly specify that a *Pastorin* should serve mainly women, children, and the inmates of hospitals and prisons. (The implications are not spelled out, but nonetheless clear!) Many *Landeskirchen* do not allow a woman to take care of the so-called "public services." A certain idea of womanhood seems to persist in the thinking of those who make the laws: the ideal type of woman for work in the church is the traditional pastor's wife as she has been pictured since the Reformation. This way of thinking has created the idea of the *Amt sui generis* (an office unique or set apart) for women. Preaching is somehow unfeminine and does not correspond to the natural place of woman in society. Therefore she may conduct a Matins service or evening devotions but not the Sunday service. Fortunately this picture obtains legally only in Thuringia and Saxony.

Third problem: the independent leadership of a congregation. The complete service to a congregation is understandably the goal of all *Vikarinnen* or women vicars. Even if they do not actually work in a parish, they all would like to have the *option* to have their own congregation if an opportunity should arise. In some *Landeskirchen* they have finally reached this goal. In others the law is more backward than the practice, and exceptions are often made. We see operating here the almost infallible law that the greater the stress and strain, the larger the need, the more flexible become attitudes and the opportunities for women in any field. This axiom explains why it is that in East Germany, where church laws are often far removed and unreflective of the realities of the situation, *and where it is against the law for women to lead a congregation,* more women pastors are employed than anywhere else. There is such a shortage of pastors that it seems ridiculous to bar women from this work.

The Church of Hannover has recently ruled to permit women pastors to assume leadership in congregations, but it has done so reluctantly in spite of the positive reaction to the use of *Vikarinnen* during the war. Only one-fourth of the *Pastorinnen* are working in parishes, and certain restrictions still obtain. For instance, there have to be at least two other pastors in a particular congregation before a *Pastorin* can be installed, which means that she may only occupy the third or fourth pastorate in a parish. Furthermore, she may apply for a pastorate in a congregation only after she has worked in a nonparish position for at least five years. In the case of men, it is often reasoned the other way around; a man should have the experience of parish work before he goes into some specialized field. Of course these laws are constantly broken and many exceptions are made. The commonly accepted attitude is "Do what is necessary, just don't talk about it!"

Fourth problem: the married Pastorin. That *Pastorinnen* may marry is a matter of considerable embarrassment to many church administrators. Old ideas of priesthood, celibacy, cultic conceptions, and many cultural attitudes toward women in general play a decisive role in this situation. Almost all *Landeskirchen* suspend the *Pastorin* in the event of her marriage. She is no longer allowed to use the title *Pastorin;* she may not wear ecclesiastical gowns; she may not conduct services; she is not permitted to preach now and then in the church of which she is a member. On this point the church law clashes with the state law, to which the church otherwise adheres in matters such as salaries, pensions, and social security. The so-called "clause of celibacy," i.e., that a contract ends in case of the marriage of the employee, has been declared inadmissible by the *Bundesarbeitsgericht* (state employment bureau), whose rulings are almost universally observed.[5] As mentioned above, the Lutheran Church of Oldenburg was the first to adopt the secular state law on this point. The Church of Hannover was the second. It seems quite clear that other district churches will gradually come around to compliance with the law. There is considerable pressure on the churches from the public as well as from the students, and, again, the shortage of academically trained workers in the church is critical; the concession will have to be made. A few churches are mentioning the possibility of married *Pastorinnen* doing part-time work. In some cases a *Pastorin* who has been widowed may be installed again, but if more than five years have passed since her last professional activity, she has to pass a colloquy conducted by the church board to qualify.

Permeating the whole discussion on the role of women in the work of the churches are uneasy questions that spring not only from the murky area of man-woman relationships (see the discussion on pp. 131-138), but also from the personal experiences of women who now work for the church. Our reports are from professional women theologians who happen to work in Germany where they have had the opportunity for wider experience in their chosen vocation. Their personal experiences are illuminating and instructive and for this reason are presented in some detail. The comments and accounts are derived from questionnaires sent to women pastors on both sides of the Iron Curtain.

To be a *Pastorin* in Germany generally means to bear a very heavy burden in many personal ways. Since there are so few *Pastorinnen* they are usually widely known and are meticulously observed both as to the quality and quantity of their work. The *Pastorin* cannot afford to do mediocre work; she must be clearly outstanding in some way to justify her position. She must always demonstrate that she is indispensable—a condition that can easily lead to neurotic feelings, and some tragedies and many sorrows can result. One gifted woman pastor committed suicide some years ago at the age of thirty-nine. It is evident that almost all *Pastorinnen* have psychological problems to overcome. Those who oppose women in the ministry argue, of course, that their problems prove the inability of women to carry such an office. But the validity of this "proof" is questionable, and the situation will probably improve the moment a *Pastorin* is no longer considered "unnatural." [6]

Since Whitsuntide, 1968, work in East Germany has become much harder for men and women pastors and all church people. The period of liberalization has come to an end. The demands and also the frustrations experienced by

A WOMAN PASTOR ANSWERS SOME PERSONAL QUESTIONS

a. *How were you accepted in the congregation?* Without any difficulty. There seemed to be no problem whatsoever in accepting a "woman in the pulpit." At first I was surprised myself. Maybe the reason is that we live in a rather even-tempered stabilized area of the church. There are here no extreme movements, no sects, no fanatical Lutherans or biblicists. . . . I am confronted with a pious stance that is positive and sustaining.

b. *How is your relationship with your colleagues?* A year ago I simply would have answered: extremely bad. Now I say: it's all right. The "bad relationship" had not primarily anything to do with my sex — at least I never noticed it — I would almost say the contrary. The basic problem is the attitude of one person to another person. For more than ten years I have been the only woman in this district. I had always imagined that ministers would be much more enjoyable and friendlier than they turned out to be. Maybe my female way of thinking led me to expect too much. At a monthly meeting of ministers a woman expects different things than men, i.e., human contact, a warm word, encouragement, a variety of topics for discussions. All this was lacking. There was hardly a friendly welcome, only hour-long debates about finances, synods, and politics — rarely pastoral problems as such.

c. *Are there disadvantages for a woman in the ministry?* By all means! It is harder for a woman and for very practical reasons. I am lucky enough to have my parents living with me. They do all the necessary housework for me. But I know *Pastorinnen* who have to do their own cooking, washing, garden work, etc. I simply can't understand how they manage. I think their health or their work must suffer in such a situation. I hope to be able to have a housekeeper if my parents can no longer do this work for me. . . . Another personal handicap for me is that I am ignorant about matters of construction. There is always something breaking down in one of our buildings and it is my job to get workers, material, and the necessary permits to repair or build. This is very hard. Nevertheless, one can do it. We managed to get the church roof repaired for fifteen thousand marks; this year the roof of the parsonage was repaired for eight thousand marks, etc. Another problem is my own sensitivity. I long for a thicker skin, the kind I notice among my colleagues. Perhaps one does tend to take everything too personally; blame and criticism hurt in a personal way. And lastly, of course, the physical capabilities of men grant them a great advantage over us. I don't take this too seriously, because it really affects all women's work. Besides, this disadvantage can be greatly reduced by toughness and energy. After three or four services on a Sunday, one after the other, I feel absolutely worn out. But some of my male colleagues feel the same.

d. *Are there any advantages over against male colleagues?* This is hard for me to judge. In any case I would say that the field of pastoral work is so wide and manifold that almost anybody, male or female, can find plenty of opportunities to exercise special talents and gifts. Naturally a man will conduct his office in a different way than a woman. But maybe the time has come to demonstrate that the line of division does not go between the sexes but rather between different talents and gifts. Generally it is said that women are better in personal contacts, such as visiting the sick, etc. But here I must confess that I am not much good in these things and I know pastors who are able to do this service in an almost perfect way. The easiest tasks for me are the general care of the congregation, preaching, and conducting congregational meetings. My special hobby is to compose songs and to use the choir as an instrument of teaching and preaching in the congregation. What I want to say is this, that I am constantly looking for those fields in which I can really make a contribution.[7]

men and women pastors will mount. The woman pastor whose answers are quoted at length doesn't mention the political stress. Nevertheless, her statements are revealing; they seem generally valid. From a very different angle she comes to the same conclusion as Dr. von Weizsäcker: that to serve the church in our day one must give up stereotyped thinking about the sexes and concentrate upon the creative use of different talents and possibilities.

A *Vikarin* from Hannover (West Germany) made, on the whole, the happiest report: her congregation petitioned for her services; she experienced no aversion in the congregation to her preaching, even though for many parishioners she was their first woman preacher. The informality of the services she conducted was especially appealing to the older people in the congregation; young people specifically asked her to marry them. She performed all the services her male counterparts did; she preached, administered the sacraments, conducted weddings and funerals, taught confirmation classes, visited the sick of both sexes. But, she was not allowed to preach in the main service or to use the pulpit because a famous preacher, Herman Bonnus, had occupied it at one time. She also pointed out that women on the staff of the church, especially the older women, occasionally created tense situations. It hurt that her advisers and superiors did not take her seriously. They felt free, for instance, to ask her on occasion to care for a busy colleague's six children.

Her most serious grievance, however, was the matter of the ceremony for ordination, which seemed to place her in a different office than a male pastor—a procedure with implications that no theologian has ever been able to explain. *"I'm afraid,"* she says, *"that we all don't really know what ordination in a Protestant church means. The word can no longer contain the Catholic concept of priesthood."*

83

Another *Pastorin* answered questions put to her about the present situation in a more sweeping way. She felt that the church outwardly and legally would make all possible concessions to women pastors now because they need them so desperately, but that a fundamental need of the church is a reshaping of the office of the pastor and the ministry of the church as a whole to modern needs. She criticized basic theological training as too narrow-minded and specialized and found in this narrowness the roots of many difficulties for women who wished to serve the church. The church, she wrote, must simply show more imagination in extending the traditional office of the ministry to a greater variety of fields than it has thus far been willing to do. She also felt that the whole debate over the service of women in the church must be freed from the idea that women and men are inevitably competing with one another. "Our final goal should never be to sit at a desk where a man has sat before and be proud to occupy his place now! In this sense a revolution in Germany against the 'established' church and its offices is inevitable and not very far off." It would be wise, she wrote, to reform the church from within before the change is forced from the outside.

In her opinion, many women working in the German churches feel that inspired and efficient use was not made of the opportunities presented by the total breakdown after World War II. *There* had been a golden opportunity to start something new; instead, there was on the whole a return to the established *Volkskirche*—with all its dusty bureaucratic structures. She feels that in the turmoil of our times a second opportunity has come to the church and now, if ever, the abilities as well as the devotion of church women must be called upon to play a creative role in reshaping the church's old ministry to serve new times.

NOTES

1. We concentrated our research on the status of women *theologians*. The experience of other full-time church workers—deaconesses, teachers, secretaries, and other assistants in the congregations and institutions of the church—is, according to our sources, not very different from their counterparts in the United States and therefore not especially instructive. Much of the information in this section was collected by Irmgard Meissner-Schulte, a German theologian who was educated in German universities, spent a year at Gustavus Adolphus College in St. Peter, Minnesota, and a year at Maywood Seminary. She served as a pastor in the Church of Hannover under Bishop Hans Lilje. She is now married to a Catholic layman, the mother of four children, and the inspired mistress of a thoroughly ecumenical household of faith.

2. The title of *Pastorin* was formally legalized by the action of the synod and the council of the United Evangelical Church of Germany in 1960.

3. It has proved somewhat difficult to get a statistical picture of the work of women theologians in the two Germanies. Figures there are; but the records produce a large variety of categories that do not match, that overlap seriously, and that leave gaps. (For instance, they do not include women theologians who work in institutions not linked directly with the church.)

4. *Frauen auf dez Kanzel? Eine brennende Frage unsere Kirche* (Stuttgart, 1967), p. 5. Quotation translated by Irmgard Meissner-Schulte.

5. According to an official publication of the Bonn government, *Die Frau im Beruf, Familie und Gesellschaft* (Bonn, 1967).

6. The prevalence of psychological problems among pastors, male and female, and in all Western countries is generally recognized and steps are being taken to alleviate some of the stresses.

7. From a questionnaire answered by an East German *Pastorin.* Translated by Irmgard Meissner-Schulte.

Chapter 8

In the
Lutheran Churches
of Scandinavia

In evaluating the role of women in the Scandinavian churches at least three major factors which they share in common must be kept in mind.[1] The Scandinavian peoples, geographically remote from Rome at the time of the expansion of the medieval church, tended to develop their own ecclesiastical practices and to modify dogma as they saw fit. The Reformation came to them, relatively painlessly, along with the profound and powerful movement toward nation-building, so the structural formation of the church and nation-state took on similar forms. The Scandinavians were more pragmatic, less revolutionary, and at the same time more free-wheeling and geared to immediate national needs than their continental counterparts. This disposition of the Scandinavian peoples has been made manifest in dozens of ways, from architecture to free love.

It pays to observe the Scandinavians because, first, they tend to represent the wave of the future; second, along with the Germans, they have bequeathed to American Lutheranism its richest and most complex heritage; and third, it seems obvious that the rapid secularization of Western people and the rapid disintegration of familiar social and political structures of all kinds will bring about in the Scandinavian countries as well as in Germany a separation of church and state. This development is forcing the churches toward radical re-formation in the structure and forms of service.

Although all of these churches have moved to ordain women and have claimed some success in the venture, it is obvious that the pressures of the state in each case were strong and that the consequence of the combination of state pressures, the novelty of the move, and the honest opposition of some church leaders (clergy especially), based avowedly on theological or biblical grounds, have led to deep divisions within the church. The main support for the ordination of women has come from women theologians, particularly the well-organized and articulate group centered around Dr. Margit Sählin, president of a church academy, the Katarina Institute, and from liberal upper-class intellectuals whose primary interest is in human rights and equality of the sexes. The congregations on the whole were considerably more receptive to women pastors than were the clergy, and rural congregations were more open-minded than the urban laboring class.

STATUS OF WOMEN PASTORS IN SWEDEN

The Church Assembly of 1957 was opposed to the ordination of women, but in the following year, 1958, a newly elected Church Assembly voted positively on the question. Most of the bishops at the time were favorable towards the ordination of women.

In the spring of 1960 the first three women theologians were ordained. The press and radio thoroughly covered these events. There are now fifteen women priests in the Lutheran Church of Sweden. Most of them are working in parishes.

Dr. Margit Sählin is the headmistress of a church academy. This academy offers many courses, conferences and retreats, and it has a good hostel for foreign and Swedish guests. Dr. Sählin also has a group of boy and girl confirmands.

Three of the other women have advanced to perpetual curates, having been elected by their parishes. All of the women priests have been met with great sympathy in the parishes and have been given great responsibility. People often come to them from other places for baptisms, weddings and funerals.

In many towns the church people and their delegates specifically want a woman priest. Unfortunately, there have been too few women theologians to ask for ordination. Most of them have become teachers in schools.

Five of our women priests are married and our laws have no restrictions in this regard.

The opposition to women priests varies in the different dioceses and it comes mostly from male priests. But most of the priests in the church are cooperating well with their women colleagues.

I have recently interviewed Archbishop Gunnar Hultgren of the Church of Sweden. The Archbishop is very sympathetic towards women priests. It is evident that he would react favorably if the American church would ordain women. He has ordained two women himself and he looks forward to the time when more women theologians will seek ordination. The Archbishop told me that, "In their parish work, seldom or never do women priests meet any opposition."[2]

Despite the rather bright picture of the status of women as pastors (priests) in Sweden, serious tensions and conflict underlie the situation. Since 1958, when the church assembly finally voted to ordain women to the priesthood, there has been no marked lessening of these tensions. Two prominent Swedish bishops are strongly opposed to ordination for women, apparently on the grounds that it is a gross manifestation of yielding to the power of secularism, a particularly clear reference to the state. A special journal has been established to represent their views. The tension has brought a serious split within the church. Those who oppose ordination speak from the position of pietism with its conservative biblical interpretation and are comparable to the Confessional group in Germany. Reporting on the thinking of representatives of this group in Sweden, an American, Eric H. Wahlstrom, lists the familiar objections raised during a meeting of the diet of the Church of Sweden in 1957: that the order of creation assigns different functions to men and women; that in his ministry the pastor represents Christ; that Jesus chose only men as apostles; that Paul forbade women to participate in church services; that the place of women in modern society is still undetermined; and that women are ineligible for apostolic succession. The matter of the apostolic succession is particularly important due to the fact that the Swedish Lutheran state church and the Anglican church base their altar and pulpit fellowship on this point. Wahlstrom suggests that the debate could be elevated considerably by bringing before the churches four issues relevant to this problem: the authority of Scripture; the nature of the ministry; the relation of church to state; and the status of women in church and society.[3]

Women priests in Sweden are generally considered *cum* pastors, i.e., associate or assistant pastors. They may not serve as chief pastors, according to an informant who visited in Sweden in the summer of 1968.

In Denmark, a startling 30 percent of the students of theology are women. Although it is assumed that most of these will be siphoned off into state schools to teach religious courses, there will likely remain a residue of women who will wish to enter the ministry.

The conflict over the ordination of women in the Danish church began shortly after women received the right to sit in parliament in 1915. In 1948, the first three women were ordained, and in 1966 there were twenty-two woman pastors, most of them in city congregations with more than one pastor. One is the only pastor in a congregation, and one is a senior pastor in a parish near Copenhagen. Some of them are married and have children. They are for the most part accepted:

> The women pastors are on quite equal terms with their male colleagues. They are allowed to apply for all clerical offices, and in their positions have the same duties, responsibility, and salaries as men. They do not feel any resistance from the congregations because they are women, but there is still quiet resistance from some male pastors. The "High Church Movement" cannot or will not acknowledge that anyone but a man can be a pastor. There may be an argument again, but it will be overcome as before.[4]

In Finland the problem of the ordination of women came up for crucial but inconclusive discussion before the assembly of the Lutheran state church in 1958. The assembly ordered a study to be made which was debated at its 1963 meeting. The Finnish church studied the question in the

---

ORDAIN WOMEN? YES. NO
1963 FINNISH CHURCH REPORT

The Recommendation: The Church Law makes no distinction between men and women with respect to ordination for the ministry. During the last decades women have assumed increasingly significant responsibilities in the Church. New times require new forms of service. The Church, too, must learn to surrender from the traditional habit of thought that the ordained ministry shall always be a man. Practically speaking, the recognition of this principle may not greatly affect the existing practices because each congregation continues to hold the right of electing its own pastor.

On the basis of Biblical and Confessional principles and in view of the practical realities we face today, this committee has the honor to propose a change in the Church Law to the effect that both men and women having properly qualified themselves may be ordained into the work of the ministry.

A certain reservation should be made with respect to the type of position to which an ordained woman is called, particularly to serve as the only full-time and wholly responsible pastor [*Kirkkoherra*, the chief pastor who carries the total responsibility for the spiritual and the material well-being of a congregation]. Only in exceptional cases shall she be authorized to hold this office.

Of the committee of five, the two women took exception to the reservation, and one male member expressed his dissenting judgment on the entire matter of ordaining women.

The Action of the 1963 Assembly: There shall be created the office of "lector." The qualifications to serve in this capacity are the same as those which pertain to the men seeking ordination. The task of the lector is to exercise sole care in the congregations, provide leadership in Christian education, and especially attend to the work among girls and women. The lector may distribute the Holy Communion according to the stipulation of the Church Law. When a woman has completed her theological studies she may request appointment as lector from the chapter of the diocese. . . .[5]

light of the New Testament, examined the problem of women and the offices of the church according to Luther and the Lutheran confessions, discussed the ordination of women in other Lutheran churches, and reexamined the office of the ministry according to church law. The 1963 assembly, acting against the recommendations of the study, created the position of lector, which was designed to resolve the problem of the ordination of women. It has not done so.

The situation in Finland is uncertain and is further complicated because clear definitions of the rights and responsibilities that adhere to the office of lector are lacking and because professionally educated women do not support the office of lector; they are campaigning for full ordination on principle even though most of them expect to serve as teachers of religion in the public schools. Congregations are said to be slow in calling lectors to serve them. One mitigating circumstance is that the deaconess movement seems to be strong in Finland and is still attracting young women who wish to serve the church.

THE ATMOSPHERE IN FINLAND—A SAMPLE

The Church Assembly is such an interesting institution that an examination of the names of the delegates inspires a song of protest from women. One can hardly admire the increase in the number of women delegates. At the 1968 Assembly there were 139 delegates, and of these 9 were women. This is 6.5 percent. In the Parliament there are 17 percent women. And yet, women play a far more active role in the Church than they do in politics.[6]

THE ATMOSPHERE IN FINLAND—A FOLKTALE

One out of two "lectors" in Helsinki is young and married. The Association of Women Theologians has expressed concern over the unemployment situation affecting women workers.

There was a "lector" who married and had children. She liked her work, her official residence was attractive, and she appreciated her income, although income tax was high. She did her work as faithfully now as she had prior to her marriage. Her patient husband and her impatient children saw her rather seldom. Never in the evenings, Saturdays or Sundays.

The children noticed that mother was home at night. Being intelligent children they worked out a scheme to see mother. They took their naps in daytime so that at night they might visit with their mother.

The "lector" lost weight, appeared pale, and soon realized that she did not know whether she belonged to the church, home, or to a rest home. Just at that time she met a young woman, recently graduated as well as married, fully prepared for the office of "lector." But she was searching for work. She had no job in the Church. These two women weighed the situation and discovered a wonderful solution to their problems: Let the "lector's" work program be divided between two workers, each one doing a part of the day.

So the employed "lector" approached her superior, the chief pastor. She was promptly informed that under law such arrangements simply could not be worked out. . . .

The overworked and fatigued "lector" continued her daily run between her work and her home, staying up late with her family. And she continues to do so this very day. And the unemployed woman continues her search for work even this day.[7]

NOTES

1. A treatment of the status of women in the state church of Norway is not included because of the general similarity to the situations in Sweden and Denmark.

2. *Lutheran Quarterly*, May 1966, p. 184. The letter was written February 2, 1966, by Märta Tamm-Götlind, at the request of the editor.

3. Eric H. Wahlstrom, "Life and Thought in World Lutheranism, Ordination of Women in the Church of Sweden?" *Lutheran Quarterly*, May 1958, pp. 161-164.

4. Hans Ollgaard, "Women as Clergymen in Denmark," *Lutheran Quarterly*, May 1966, p. 167.

5. These abstracts from the Minutes of the 1963 Assembly of the Church of Finland were made available to Dr. J. W. Heikkinen, a

member of the commission, through the courtesy of Archbishop Simojoki of the Church of Finland. Translated by Dr. Heikkinen.

6. Riitta Virkkunen in *Vartija,* May 1968, p. 213. Translated by J. W. Heikkinen.

7. Leena Ormio, "Folktale About Women Workers in the Church," *Vartija,* January 1969, p. 35. Translated by J. W. Heikkinen.

Chapter 9

In the
Lutheran Churches
of North America

That the churches of all Western countries are in a state of crisis is clear. From the local parishes to the national bureaucracies of the separate denominations and their national and international ecumenical bodies, the alarms have been rung: decrease in membership, the disaffection of youth, the falling off of financial support, the drop in seminary enrollment and the disinclination of many seminarians to enter the parish ministry, greater demands for an ever-broadening service to secular society just at the point when resources in money and personnel are weakening, the pressing need for reinterpretation of the basic tenets of faith under the burden of the massive turbulence in the world—all of this, and more.

But shafts of light are beginning to penetrate the gloom. First of all, there is a good chance that the pilgrim church, lean and sparse, will once again as so often in the past take up its burdens with heightened hope. We can find hope in the extraordinary experiences of the church in the World War II period, whose monumental tragedies put Lutherans on both sides of the conflict and on both sides of the Iron Curtain in bondage. Contrite and innovative, some churches undertook to face a new time. New structures, new ministries—including those of women—new concepts of the role of the laity in the life of the European churches were developed. Their problems deeply involved the American churches during the fifties. Now that a time of troubles is upon the American churches in the seventies, it is reasonable to hope that the resourcefulness and resilience learned in Europe a generation ago may be called upon. There is also considerable reason to believe that the voices of church leaders are being heard in the hinterland; that the gap between enlightened church leadership and the local parishes seems to be closing. Seminaries are showing signs of responding creatively to the demands for radically new kinds of ministries. But, most important of all, *the problems are being brought into the light of day.*

Among the problems that are emerging is, of course, the woman problem, and the impact of it is being felt throughout the church. It is useless to bemoan the annoying persistence of this issue. It is equally futile to affirm: "If we get bogged down in *this* debate, we cannot cope with our other, more urgent problems" or "The ecumenicity we need will be gravely threatened." These are valid and predictable reactions, but they contain no constructive promise. They are mentioned here only because along with the Roman Catholic and Anglican churches, the Lutherans have been late in facing the problem and have traditionally held the most conservative position.[1] The congregations need to know that these laments have been heard before among our brethren and do not spring solely from a unique and present anguish.

As short a time as four years ago, it was possible for a Lutheran churchman in an editorial to describe the woman problem in our churches as the "greatest 'hidden' problem in our midst" and to call upon "the Lutheran denominations, dominated as they are by male clergy . . ." to ". . . first of all acknowledge the scandal in our midst. . . ." It can now at least be said that the problem is no longer hidden. The problem as problem is recognized; the proportions of

THE MINISTRY OF WOMEN—AN EDITORIAL

It may well be that the role of women in the Lutheran churches is the greatest "hidden" problem in our midst today. We have many problems, to be sure, several of which are more important than the role of women. But they are out in the open——the ecumenical challenge, the churches' role in the civil rights movement, the churches' attitude towards secularity, etc. But there seems to be some massive tendency to push under the rug the issue of women's place in the churches, to table the discussion for some indeterminate future time. Ask about the role of women and the response is likely to be smiles and snickers, or devoutly serious assertions that "no one is interested in pursuing that issue."

However, one must ask whether there is any other issue which we Lutherans in North America are more inadequately prepared to discuss. Let us look at the place of women in the ministry of our churches. We have deaconesses, parish workers, directors of Christian education, campus workers, and other types of positions for women. Yet, there is probably no more insecure group of God's servants than these women. They have reason to feel insecure. If the congregational budget has to be cut, these women will be the first to be "eased out," in order to trim costs. Leading men in the churches, including members of deaconess boards, have in the past indicated that they seek to eliminate full-time women workers, except for secretaries and other "non-religious" positions. Sometimes pastors have even blurted out the opinion that "only the most physically attractive, gifted women should be recruited for the churches' work." And, most ironically, a clergy that is ridden with its own neuroses and maladjustments complains that women who have their own "personal problems" ought to seek to serve outside the church, in the "world where they belong." These attitudes are all too common, and they should be recognized for the cruel, often subchristian attitudes they conceal.

Of course, there are some who try to rectify these sad conditions for the wrong reasons. They are the feminists, who demand equal rights for women, as a correlate to secular feminism, simply because women constitute over half of our membership. "Equal rights" usually means ordination The real issue for us Lutherans, however, is not whether we can support a feminist movement within our precincts. The real question is whether the Lutheran churches have the spirit and the vision, the quality of piety, not to mention the corporate structure, that can receive and integrate into our common life the zeal for full-time service that animates many of our fellow Christians who happen to be women. There is no doubt at all that at the present time the Lutheran denominations must answer this question in the negative.

Until we recognize the scandal in our treatment of full-time women workers in the churches and acknowledge our inadequacies in providing them opportunities for service, we cannot fulfill our calling as communities of love and concern and diaconic ministry. This does not mean that we will rush to ordain women into our ministry of Word and sacrament. It means, first of all, that we will reassess the whole area of lay service in our churches, and try to integrate the distinctively feminine roles of service into our ministry as God's peope. It means that we will restore to our women their full civil liberties in our midst including adequate salaries, working conditions, terms of tenure, etc.). We will not be able to avoid the question of ordination of women, it is true. Before we can tackle this question, however, some important nonfeminist considerations must be given careful thought. Perhaps the most important of these is the ecumenical question.

In the ecumenical perspective, we must weigh very seriously the effect that our ordination of women would have on other Christians. Would the ordination of women in our denominations be as irresponsible and offensive, ecumenically, as the promulgation of the Marian dogmas by the Roman church? Some of the most significant groups of Christians do not now ordain women, and the prospects are dim that they will begin the practice in the foreseeable future. These groups find some support for their refusal to ordain women in Scripture, although that support is hotly contested by some scholars. Nevertheless, do we wish to prejudice future cooperation with these churches by action now, to ordain women?

It is unlikely that we will feel a need to ordain women in the near future.[2] It is much more important to find ways to integrate women into the non-ordained ministries of our denominations, just as it is highly important that we integrate all laymen—male and female—into these ministries. The years ahead should be ones of reassessment for American Lutherans as they consider the shape of their ministry. The place of women in that ministry cannot be ignored much longer. The Lutheran denominations, dominated as they are by male clergy, must first of all acknowledge the scandal in our midst; then they must proceed under the judgment and inspiration of evangelical criteria to resolve the issues that have caused that scandal.[3]

it are beginning to be grasped; it has found its place on the agenda of deliberative bodies; fact-finding studies are underway. Every Lutheran body is presently studying the woman problem, and the Lutheran Council in the U.S.A. (which includes the American Lutheran Church, the Lutheran Church–Missouri Synod, and the Lutheran Church in America) has a joint research and study project now underway.

It is also significant that on international ecumenical levels, women are seeking larger responsibilities. For instance, forty women from eighteen countries participated in a week-long deliberation in Bastad, Sweden, the first in a series of conferences preceding the 1970 Lutheran World Federation Fifth Assembly.[4] The purpose of the conference was to define the Christian responsibility of women in a technical, pluralistic, and political world through which, inevitably, women will advocate a stronger role in the decision-making units of the LWF. It was pointed out that of a total of seventy-three persons on the federation's executive committee and its seven principal commissions, there are only three women. Among the LWF's nearly thirty executives in Geneva, one woman holds a top position.

The always prominent ecumenical and international interests of Lutheran women were demonstrated at this conference in Bastad. Nearly half the participants came from the "Third World" of the have-not nations, one-fifth were consultants and observers from non-Lutheran churches: Anglican, Methodist, Reformed, and Roman Catholic.

THE LUTHERAN CHURCH IN AMERICA

The first promising overt sign that the Lutheran Church in America was ready to face the woman problem was the fact that the LCA Commission on the Comprehensive Study of the Doctrine of the Ministry, appointed in 1964, found it possible to include a discussion of the matter in its report to the biennial convention of 1966. This commission's enlightened and moderate views as to the necessity for the church to open up opportunities for qualified women in positions of greater responsibility laid the foundation for the work of the present commission.

Their statement precipitated a lively, agitated, and at times acrimonious debate, which centered heavily on the projected image of the parish pastor, which doubtless would be affected by any serious recognition of women in the higher brackets of professional church workers. The discussion focused, naturally enough, on the problem of ordination, in spite of the commission's emphasis on non-ordained ministries which should be created by the church and open to both sexes to make the church's service to society more relevant to clamant and shifting needs. The discussion nevertheless did lay open complications and concerns which led the convention to direct the appointment of the present commission with a specific charter to

REPORT TO THE 1966 LCA CONVENTION

In one sense it is unnecessary to speak of any "special" role of women in the ministry of the church, "for as many of you as were baptized into Christ have put on Christ. There is . . . neither male nor female; for you are all one in Christ Jesus" (Gal. 3:27-28). However, there are obvious biological differences between male and female and as well distinctions in cultural roles assigned according to sex. These factors do not nullify the Pauline insight into the baptismal equality of the sexes, but rather this insight leads to an awareness that there is continual need for re-examination of all stereotyped cultural and social differences between man and woman, to determine those that are relative and outmoded and consequently irrelevant and even harmful to the church's ministry.

This is not merely to further the emancipation of the modern woman. More important is the desire that no artificial or unrealistic limitations be placed upon the Christian woman's call to minister. This desire, together with a candid acknowledgment that the church has not always accorded equal opportunity or responsibility to its woman members, makes it necessary to stress not only the baptismal equality of the sexes, but also the need for the church to develop within her total structure opportunities for women to minister commensurate with their abilities.

Some churches within world Lutheranism have decided that the development of such outlets includes the opening of ordination for women. At present in this church there is neither theological nor social consensus on this question, and there has not been sufficient time or study given to warrant a final decision now. However, since ordination of women is an open question in American Lutheranism, and a seriously discussed matter in many Lutheran churches, it seems reasonable to recommend, as we do, that in the future this church study the question in depth.[5]

study the problem of the ordination of women. The action indicated clearly that the officials and a substantial number of the representatives of the church would press on toward a resolution of the problems of the ministry, the laity, the role of women, and ordination. These events reflected serious concern which had been building up in many quarters of the church, particularly since the late fifties, and clearly put the LCA in the front ranks of the Lutheran churches in America in seeking new approaches to old problems.

In its progress report to the 1968 convention the commission announced that it could find no theological or biblical reasons for denying ordination to women; that, were ordination denied to women, the grounds would be found in the social, cultural, psychological, and biological areas. It has been generally expected that the LCA would be first among the Lutheran churches in the United States to be confronted by the problem, for there were enrolled in the various seminaries of the church in the fall of 1969 about two dozen women students who have stated their intention to qualify for certification for ordination.[6] In May 1969, a group of twenty-five seminarians from various institutions met to discuss matters of theological education, including the ordination of women, and the reports of the meeting indicated that these students would support such certification. Should ordination be denied these women, it seems quite clear that their professional skills will not be put to the service of the church in the diaconate, but will be used either by special ministries or be "lost" to the church by diversion to secular organizations.

In other areas there are signs that the LCA is recognizing the urgency of the "woman problem." The LCA is, of course, cooperating with the Lutheran Council in the U.S.A. in its study on the ordination of women. LCA Vocational

Services has upgraded the employment and personnel practices of the church so that the church as an employer will give proper recognition to professional training without discrimination on the basis of sex.[7] In its unpublished "Status Study," LCAVS claims that ". . . the church must keep abreast of the times. The church is an innovator in all life stages of the social complex." In its publication, *LCA Plan for Church Occupations,* it is at least implied that except for the positions of pastor and deaconess there are no restrictions on the basis of sex in matters of rank, salary, vacations, fringe benefits, etc. Lutheran Church Women is one of thirteen church bodies represented on the Coordinating Committee on Church Vocations; two women serve on the three-man Vocational Service Staff, one as director of registry and placement, the other as executive secretary.

But at the synodical level of the LCAVS structure the name of not one woman appears as chairman or as staff official. In view of the recognized need for more women in church vocations, it is significant that of the 353 Lutherans who serve on the church vocations committees of the 33 synods of the church, only 27 are women. (This group includes four psychologists.) The 27 are concentrated in 17 of the 33 synods. Furthermore, except for references to the program for deaconesses and the associates in deaconess service, no special pitch is made for the recruitment of women for whom many of the categories of jobs would be deemed appropriate, and the material in the handbooks and in the proposed films does not deal with the special handicaps the church labors under in the recruitment of women.

These handicaps were amply spelled out for our commission in its interviews with ten undergraduate women students who were preparing for church vocations and one of their teachers. The atmosphere of these sessions was friendly, relaxed, even gay, yet the basic note could only be called grim. The women acknowledged right away that the problems of marriage and children were formidable, but could see no reason why in many vocations within the church the same adjustment made in secular vocations to accommodate career women could not also be made by the church. They considered the major stumbling blocks to be the attitudes of their local pastors, who thought exclusively in traditional terms of the missionary, the parish worker, the diaconate, nursing in church-related institutions, and church secretarial work. Other church officials, their own parents—who in most cases are faithful church members who uniformly opposed their going into dead-end and poorly rewarded church work—and the total disregard of church work as a proper vocational choice either for men or women constituted further blocks.

About half the young women interviewed were not interested in ordination for themselves, although they felt that the question should remain an open one. To a woman they felt strongly that some such title as "associate" and not always that of "assistant" should be available to them if they qualified for certain jobs. They resented the inequities in working conditions, salaries, and security provisions prevalent in the church. They complained that there were few excellent "majors" in religious education available, that career possibilities were not publicized, that their interviews with the church vocation committees of synods were "dismal," and that even the social affairs arranged for students of both sexes were geared entirely toward men. They, as women, heard from these committees only about the diaconate. They suggested specifically that opportunities for work within the church be clearly announced to high-school girls and to their parents, and especially that the different varieties of service open to women in suburban, inner-city, small-town, and rural communities be precisely described.

Much more trenchant, incisive, and wide-ranging were the written evaluations of their careers and personal experiences in working for the church made at the request of the commission by nine experienced and professionally educated women. All nine women are members of congregations; all nine *have* worked for the church or are at present employed by the churches; two are deaconesses; two are social workers; two are teachers; one is a counselor to students in a campus ministry; one is an executive in a national ecumenical office; one is a professional writer. To these women ordination in itself is not the critical issue; they do not consider the deep and pervasive frustrations that accompany inspired and dedicated work on behalf of the church to be completely unbearable. But the basic issue is one of justice, recognition, and the opportunity to work at full competence and in communal fellowship. Besides discrimination in salary, vacations, secretarial help, and retirement benefits, these women are psychologically burdened by attitudes, practices, and structures that are culturally archaic and theologically questionable and which, in their opinion, are depriving the church of full effectiveness in its work for our time and our society.[8]

At the heart of the matter, in short, they see not the role of women *per se* in the leadership and services of the church, but the role of men and women *together* in Christian community, living and working in the common faith we affirm. About half the women specifically mentioned the potentiality of team ministries. The loneliness of ministry within the church has been a common complaint of its servants, both male and female, for a long time. So serious is the problem for clergymen that special counseling has been made available to them by the church. It is obvious that the problem of isolation and loneliness is even more grave for women.

The professional women consulted by the commission do not ask for favors or concessions; but they ask that they, too, may be considered as intelligent human beings with talents and abilities and that their competence and ambition be respected. All the women accepted almost as a matter of course that larger demands would be made upon them than upon their male counterparts and that their margin for error would be less. Some of the most able women among them have found that their professional experience and competence actually counts against them eventually, because the positions for which they would otherwise qualify are closed to them *as women*. However incisive their criticism, their judgments were benevolent, their tone restrained. Nevertheless, the majority had left the service of the church. The weight of their sentiments, perhaps, could be summed up in a quote from one of the most astute observers of women and the church: "If organized religion rises to the present challenge, the centuries ahead may yet turn out to be something more nearly what the Lord had in mind when he took the trouble to create a world and—hopefully—a responsible human race, not two divided and bickering sexes."[9]

This much said, it is not clear how the whole community called the Lutheran Church in America regards the role of women in the church. The national leaders have led the way toward the exploration of fuller opportunities for women. But even if the church should permit women to be ordained, there is no clear indication of general acceptance. The experience of the German and the Scandinavian churches is instructive but not definitive, of course. The commission made a beginning in sounding out the thinking of the church by addressing a questionnaire to all presidents of synods. All thirty-one responded.[10] Their responses varied in tone and mood from the serious, urbane, and thoughtful to the equally serious, somewhat irascible, and firmly fundamentalist posture that asserts that women should stay where they belong and that mothers working outside the home make a major contribution to juvenile delinquency, etc. Although the questionnaire invited the presidents to evaluate the role of women in many tasks that do *not* require ordination, the specter, threat, or promise of the consequences of ordination for women pervaded the answers returned by them.

All thirty-one of the presidents said that to their knowledge the role of women in the life of the church had never come up for discussion within their synods. Of these, eighteen said that no women had completed academic studies which, had they been men, would have qualified them for ordination. One woman had been so qualified in each of six synods; two women in each of two synods; three in each of two synods; and three additional presidents indicated that there possibly had been at least one woman so qualified. Of the nineteen women involved, not one, according to the reports, had seriously applied for ordination, although several presidents indicated that several women had recently announced their intention to do so.

In answer to the question about women conducting regular church services in public, sixteen presidents reported that to their knowledge no women had done so in their synods. Ten presidents reported that women had preached in *regular* services. Five reported that women had preached at five *special* services; one reported that a woman had preached and also conducted the liturgy at several public services with surprisingly good response; two reported that wives of pastors had either read or preached sermons on two occasions. In only one out of the eighteen cases that

EXCERPTS FROM LCA SYNOD PRESIDENTS' RESPONSES

I do not consider it hazardous to the progress of *ecumenism* to consider the ordination of women, though it might be hazardous to inter-Lutheran relations were we to sanction ordination of women at this time. Obviously, we have to recognize that LC — MS has not even begun to grant women suffrage in the church, not even at the congregational level.[11] Neither ALC or LCA has any well-developed pattern for recognizing the equality of women in the church, witness the composition of church councils, convention delegations, board membership, etc.

It is difficult to say with certainty that the LCA's traditional stance toward the ordination of women "has deprived the church of valuable service," but I believe that it has in many instances. I could name at least four highly gifted women from this sector of the church who would have prepared for ordination had that avenue of service been open to them. Each has made a valuable contribution to the work of the church in her present vocation — as teacher, writer, homemaker, etc. But I believe that each could have made a strong contribution as an ordained minister, perhaps a more distinctive and valuable contribution than she is currently making.

Unless the church provides more significant leadership roles for women I believe that many of our most thoughtful, sensitive and articulate women will become progressively alienated from the male-oriented, male-dominated structures of the church. Except for men who serve the church professionally, I find few other men who show the developed sensitivity to social and spiritual concerns evidenced by many thoughtful women, few men who are as willing to devote themselves to study, thought and active leadership in the church as women.

108

We men have been making the decisions and writing the rules in the church long enough. I think that it's time that we actualize Paul's saying, that in Christ "there is neither male nor female," but that all are equally called to and eligible for service in the Church.

Clearly, if our sights are set at an eventual merger of all Lutheran bodies in the United States then LCA action favorable to ordination of women would damage such progress. However, there is pretty clear evidence available (seemingly ignored by most of the LCA leadership) that the pastors and people of the Lutheran Church in America are more similar in their attitudes, behavior, and church life to Presbyterians than they are to Missouri Synod Lutherans. I think it is fairly certain that COCU[12] will approve ordination of women.

I would certainly expect that trends in American society will continue toward acceptance of women on an equal status with men in many occupations and professions, and I am convinced that a fully developed sense of a team ministry would require on a team competently trained women, ordained or unordained. I would have difficulty justifying lack of ordination, which would imply a "second-rate status" to women because of the accidents of their biological make-up.

I see turmoil in the churches and in the world as an argument against women being associated with leadership responsibility. They don't lack courage or creativity. But physiology and psychology still seem to indicate that they are in some ways "weaker vessels."

I hope members of your committee have more insight into this concern than I have. I can't conceive of any valid reason that absolutely prevents ordination for women. Yet I can't convince myself that it would be good for the church. I churn at the increasing number of church councils with women members — not at the women but at the associated explanation, "We couldn't get men to take the job."

If we get in trouble, circumstances may force us to take similar action [i.e., in *crisis*, as in Germany after World War II.][13]

---

were reported in any detail was there any indication of a negative reaction to a woman having participated in the service in these ways.

"*What would be your response as the President of an LCA Synod to a request for ordination from a woman who was fully qualified?*" Thirteen answered "no"; twelve answered "yes"; three were uncertain; nine would in any case regardless of their personal views refer the matter to higher church officials and/or wait until the church had spoken. One president felt that any action at all would be premature. Ten presidents based their thinking, whether pro or con, on theological grounds primarily; five on legal or constitutional grounds (these were all negative); nine on practicality and expediency; and one on psychological-biological grounds. Needless to say, this last one was a negative vote. Five presidents specifically advocated intensive further study of the problem of women's role in the church. Thirteen presidents felt that even the *consideration* of the ordination of women was hazardous either to ecumenism in general or to inter-Lutheran cooperation or both. Six felt that the church should proceed to do what is just and right regardless of the risk to ecumenical progress; ten felt that there were no substantial hazards involved that could not be overcome within a reasonable time.

Twenty-six presidents said that regardless of their view on ordination for women, they were not aware of any instances in which the church's traditional stance had deprived it of valuable services. Four presidents cited instances to the contrary. Twenty-one presidents were very sure that the present turmoil within our churches and throughout society would notably enlarge the role played by women in the life of the church. Four felt that the role of women would not change. Six did not wish to make a judgment on the matter.

An analysis of the returns from the questionnaires seems to justify the conclusion that however obscure much of the picture is at the congregational and synodical levels, the presidents are on the whole receptive to the idea that women should be allowed and even encouraged to serve in the church in other than their traditional roles. It is certainly significant that one-third of them have indicated their willingness to ordain women. But there is little evidence at either the synodical or congregational levels that the role of women in the church is being seriously discussed. There is manifest only great restiveness under the present situation, and further erosion of resources and personnel will doubtless take place. The education of the clergy and the laity of the LCA toward an enlightened consideration of the "woman problem" obviously rests at this point in the hands of national officers, their boards and task forces, and with seminaries. At least one seminary, the Hamma School of Theology, has recruited women students with the deliberate intention of creating what it considers to be a normal community for dialog within the seminary. In its new curriculum it is looking forward to a time when women may be recruited more extensively for professional work in the church.

THE AMERICAN LUTHERAN CHURCH

It probably is fairly accurate to say that the general position of the American Lutheran Church vis-à-vis the woman problem is to the right of what is presumed to be the position of the Lutheran Church in America and to the left of the Lutheran Church—Missouri Synod. Women of the ALC are not active in policy-making bodies of the church and in some congregations, probably a minority, women may not vote. However, there is a constitutional provision that women may serve on two of the boards of the church in addition to those that deal exclusively with women's work.[14] Since the constitution is also under study this opportunity (or restriction) may be revised. Women may be sent as delegates both to district conventions and the general convention of the church.

As is true of other Lutheran bodies, ordination in the ALC has been reserved for men, and the matter of ordination for women has only recently come up for review. In recent years women have attended ALC seminaries, but most of them received degrees in religious education and served as parish workers or as directors of Christian education. A few years ago, however, several women students at the ALC's Luther Theological Seminary in St. Paul, Minnesota, announced that they wished the faculty to consider them as candidates for certification for ordination, and on October 30, 1968, the faculty adopted a position paper supporting the recommending of qualified women theological students for ordination.

Two of the three candidates were indeed so certified. One has accompanied her husband who has already been ordained to serve a parish in Colorado; the other has been called as assistant pastor to a parish in North Dakota. The

---

ALC SEMINARY POSITION PAPER ON ORDAINING WOMEN

Four sets of objections are urged against the ordination of women to the ministry: biblical, theological, practical, and ecumenical.

1. The New Testament does not confront the question of ordination of women and therefore does not speak directly to it. On the other hand, nothing in the New Testament speaks decisively against it.

2. Although the ordination of women raises new and difficult questions, there is no decisive theological argument against the ordination of women.

3. The practical objections, however serious, do not by themselves settle the question for Lutherans. As long as no decisive biblical or theological objections are raised, the ordination of women remains a possibility.

4. The most serious objection is the ecumenical, that Lutherans ought not unilaterally in the present divided state of Christendom make decisions which affect all Christian churches. But inasmuch as other churches already have ordained women to the ministry, and some churches not presently ordaining women are open to discussion of its possibility, the exact weight of this objection is difficult to assess.

In view of the considerations above, we can see no valid reason why women candidates for ordination who meet the standards normally required for admission to the ministry should not be recommended for ordination.[15]

---

matter of her ordination has been referred to the Lutheran Council in the U.S.A. by the governing body of the ALC, the church council. According to a report in *The Lutheran,* LCUSA's Division of Theological Studies has taken the position that ". . . ordination for women was neither conclusively forbidden nor demanded by biblical doctrine, but urged church bodies to 'act only after consultation with fellow Lutherans.' "[16]

The thinking of the ALC council is perhaps best carried in a statement from the minutes of its meetings in the summer of 1964:

> Since the ministerial office is not precisely defined in the New Testament and since the duties of early officers were varied and interchangeable, and since the needs of the Church down through the centuries are subject to variation, we are led to Luther's conclusion; namely, that God has left the details of the ministerial office to the discretion of the church, to be developed according to its needs and according to the leading of the Holy Spirit.[17]

On the basis of the council's statement, three members of the faculty of the ALC's Wartburg Theological Seminary prepared a paper entitled, "Preliminary Theses on the Ministry and Ordination," which was received by the council but which, so far as we know, has no particular standing within the church. Two of the five theses might possibly affect the conditions under which women could offer a professional ministry in the ALC. Thesis 4 reads: "The authority to define a particular ministry, and to call and commission a person to it, rests with the people of God at any given place or in connection with a specific territorial or organizational responsibility." In support of this thesis, the three faculty members state: "The door must not be closed to the commissioning of a woman to *any* function within the church to which a man might be commissioned." Thesis 5 reads: "If maximum opportunity for change and freedom is given God's people under the guidance of the Spirit, we can be assured that the Spirit will not only give the church the ministers required for our day but will also preserve order and discipline." Regarding the ordained ministry, they say, "In our present system, the seminary faculty and the church council (synod) rule on the qualifications of the candidate for ordination. Under the greater freedom of the proposed plan, any recognized congregation could call a person to a particular function and ask that his name be placed on the professional roster of synod." This information furnished among LCUSA papers given the commission helps give an indication of the expanding and creative consideration being given to the "woman problem" in the American Lutheran Church.

THE LUTHERAN CHURCH—MISSOURI SYNOD

The debate over the role its women members shall play in the affairs of this the most conservative of the major Lutheran bodies is getting very lively. But the crucial issue at this time is the matter of women voting in congregational meetings. The synod has been debating the issue intermittently for a century, but the matter has not become urgent until the last decade. Until 1969 only 10 percent of the Missouri Synod congregations had allowed women to *attend* voters' meetings; 5 percent had allowed women to serve on congregational boards or committees, but not to vote. One percent of the congregations had permitted women to vote on important congregational matters.[18] The sticking points for many years have been Paul's famous dictum that women shall be silent in church and the rule that, under no condition, should they "usurp authority over men." Should women achieve a voting majority this rule could be considered violated.

Strong efforts have come from several quarters to bring the church to grant the vote to women and to enlarge their opportunities for service in the church beyond the highly circumscribed and traditional functions. One of these is the prestigious editorial board of *Cresset,* a journal published by Valparaiso University; another is a number of scholarly and progressive young clergymen, teachers, and professional theologians—of that remarkable quality that has always distinguished this church—who are reexamining Scripture in the light of the current crises within and outside the church. Still another source of restiveness is a strong grass-roots movement among the younger congregations, particularly in the South and Southwest.[19]

At their national convention in Denver, Colorado, in July 1969, the church representatives voted to allow women to vote in the congregations. Each congregation, however, has the right to decide whether it will allow its women to vote. (One can't help wondering whether the *viva voce* rule may not be disallowed!) The pastoral office is specifically withheld.

The basic position taken by the church is best described in a set of declarations presented to the church council at its 1969 convention in a report of the church's Commission on Theology and Church Relations. These declarations clearly manifest the view that the exercise of the franchise by women, as well as by men, is now considered to be an opportunity for *service* to the church. But the holding of *any* office in the church at *any* level that would empower a woman to exercise authority over men would constitute a violation of the order of creation. This stricture would apply specifically to the pastoral office and membership on the board of elders.

The order of creation is considered inviolable because it protects the institution of matrimony and establishes for once and all the question of authority in the home. It is stated again and again in the literature of the church that there is no inference of the inferiority of the woman in this ordering, for Christ was subordinate to God, and Christ rejoiced in this subordination. So should the Christian woman rejoice and gladly serve under the authority of her husband at home, and under male members of the church in its congregations and offices.

LC—MS DECLARATIONS ON WOMEN'S RIGHTS

1. We find nothing in Scripture which prohibits women from exercising the franchise in voters' assemblies.

2. Those statements of Scripture which direct women to keep silent in the church, and which prohibit them to teach and to exercise authority over men, we understand to mean that women ought not to hold the pastoral office.

3. Such passages, we hold, indicate that women ought not to hold any other office in the church whose function it is to assist the pastor in the exercise and administration of the Office of the Keys.

4. The principles set forth in such passages, we believe, apply also to holding any other kind of office in the institutional structures of the church which might involve women in a violation of the order of creation.

5. We find no statement in Scripture which prohibits women from holding office on the boards and committees of Synod whether such offices are filled by election or by appointment.

6. We conclude that the Synod itself and the congregations of the Synod are at liberty to alter their constitutions and their practices to conform to these declarations if they believe that such changes are in the best interest of the congregation and of the church at large.[20]

NOTES

1. Among the Lutheran churches before the merger in 1963, the old United Lutheran Church in America seemed to have been among the first to have opened up to women membership in several of its major boards with the notable exception of the executive board. As late as 1953, however, there were still no women on special committees and commissions. A few women served as delegates to the national convention, and to the National Lutheran Council, the National Council of Churches, and the World Council of Churches. Ten years later, in 1963, Nona M. Diehl, reporting on Lutheran women's work around the world after the merger of 1963, noted that there was an increase in the number of women working in eleven familiar categories of deaconess work. About 350 women were active in missionary, healing, or educational work, and as staff members on boards of the church doing writing and editing, field work, and conducting leadership training and recruiting programs for church vocations. Two women were by this time serving on the executive board of the LCA and there were twenty-four women serving on eight boards and seven commissions of the church. There were, however, few women theologians in North America in general, and the small number of Lutheran women who received the Bachelor of Divinity degree earned it in other than Lutheran seminaries. Nona M. Diehl, *Lutheran Women Around the World* (Philadelphia: Board of Publication of the Lutheran Church in America, 1963), pp. 49-53.

2. *The Christian Century*, April 28, 1963, p. 1053, listed sixty women considered theologians. Of these, five were Lutherans. How many more names could be added to this list we do not know. But there are at least thirty to forty Lutheran women studying theology in degree-earning programs. We do not know how many have serious intentions to strive for ordination. Editor's note.

3. Philip J. Hefner, "The Ministry of Women." In a letter to the author dated March 4, 1970, Dr. Hefner offered the following clarifying statement to his editorial: "I would intensify today the critique of our church's inability and unwillingness to recognize the ministry of women at every level of the church's life. The editorial was erroneously interpreted by some as opposing the ordination of women and as a criticism of militant spokesmen for women's rights. On the contrary, I was rather attempting to say that it is not only the ordination of women, but their treatment generally that needs to be reassessed by the church and reoriented.

4. In July 1970 in Brazil.

5. Lutheran Church in America, Report of the Commission on the Comprehensive Study of the Doctrine of the Ministry, Appendix A, "Women in the Ministry of the Church," pp. 618-619.

6. The following table was prepared for the commission subcommittee by Mildred E. Winston, consultant to the executive secretary of the Board of Theological Education.

LCA Women Students at Theological Seminaries
Working in Degree Programs 1969/70

LCA Seminaries					
Seminary	*BD/MDiv*	*MA/MAR*	*Grad*	*Uncl.*	*Total*
Chicago	2	5			7
Gettysburg	1	4		1	6
Hamma	5				5
Northwestern				2	2
Pacific	1	1	1		3
Philadelphia	1	2		2	5
Saskatoon		1			1
Southern		2			2
Waterloo	1				1
Total	11	15	1	5	32

Non-Lutheran Seminaries					
Seminary	*BD/MDiv*	*MA/MAR*	*Grad*	*Uncl.*	*Total*
Chicago	2				2
Harvard		1			1
New York	1			2	3
Princeton		1			1
Union (NY)		1			1
Yale		3			3
Total	3	6	0	2	11

7. An administrative unit of the Board of College Education and Church Vocations, the LCAVS has mapped out a program of recruitment and career training of professional workers for the church. The basic program is to be implemented by the thirty-three synod committees on church vocations.

8. For both deaconesses, for instance, the garb seemed a real barrier to communication both inside and outside the church.

9. Culver, *Women in the World of Religion,* p. 232.

10. Divisions of two synods, New York and Eastern Pennsylvania, since the survey was taken in 1968 have increased the number of LCA synods to thirty-three. Not all presidents answered all questions.

11. The Lutheran Church—Missouri Synod did, however, vote to allow women to vote in their congregations under most circumstances. See pp. 115-117. Editor's note.

12. COCU is the Consultation on Church Union, an interdenominational body. Editor's note.

13. From unpublished questionnaires sent out to presidents of LCA synods by the commission.

14. Diehl, *Lutheran Women Around the World,* p. 53.

15. This document was obtained through the courtesy of the president of the seminary.

16. *The Lutheran,* July 2, 1969, p. 23.

17. ALC Council Minutes, June 26-27, July 1-2, 1964, commission exhibit J-3, sec. B, 7.

18. These figures are based on returns from questionnaires mailed to presidents of the Missouri Synod's districts in 1965 by the *Reporter,* an LC–MS magazine.

19. In all fairness it should be noted for the critics of the churches in this matter of suffrage that the vote was not given to women until 1920 and the equalizing of voting privileges for men and women was accomplished only in 1928. In Switzerland, generally considered one of the most liberal countries in the world, women still do not have the franchise in some cantons. In others they could probably have the franchise but do not want it.

20. The Lutheran Church—Missouri Synod, Report of the Commission on Theology and Church Relations, *Woman Suffrage and the Church* (Saint Louis, n.d.), p. 3.

Part III

Basic
Problems of
Emancipation

Chapter 10

Ordination

BIBLICAL AND THEOLOGICAL CONSIDERATIONS

Whenever the role of women in the work of the church is discussed, concern quickly centers on the problem of ordination. What is ordination? By what authority does the church speak on ordination? Who may be ordained and for what?

Now it is the business of theologians to instruct the church on these matters. But they are divided and the debate rolls on—as it must! There are those who stand on the authority of Scripture in the strict sense that certain passages are interpreted literally to support their case. This stance is very often thought to be in the Protestant and especially the Lutheran tradition. This school is encumbered by the fact that "there are very few, if any statements for which with a little ingenuity one could not find apparent biblical support so long as one is content to treat the Bible as a collection of proof texts."[1] There are those theologians who take their task to mean that they must communicate to the people of God the content of received doctrine so stated by the church for two thousand years. This is often taken to be the Catholic position. Then there is a third position taken by those theologians who consider their task to be to understand the will and mind of God as he reveals his will and mind in his acts of creation and redemption continuously in the world he created and is still creating. This school of theologians recognizes that their insights are conditioned by the culture of their time and that as conditions of life change so must certain of their insights. They have the difficult task of trying to identify through the study of the Bible and the work of generations of theologians what is genuine insight and what might be a misreading of the message "due to their having the outlook of their time and place."[2] But in spite of all hazards God calls his people always to a deeper understanding of what he has done and is doing, and it is clear that his action is both creative and redemptive.

It is the challenging and awesome task of the ordained minister to preach the Word, administer the sacraments, and serve the congregation under an inspired and studied comprehension of God's Word in the contemporary theater of action.

Now we confront the question head-on: Must this ministry be restricted to males? There are four arguments that are always presented to sustain the theological objections to the ordination of women: 1) that Christ chose only men to be apostles; 2) that God and Christ are masculine and thus a priest must also be; 3) that women by nature are unable to receive the "indelible character" conferred by ordination; and 4) that God has ordained for all time the subordination of women. The first three of these arguments are set forth and answered very clearly by the Reverend Leonard Hodgson, D.D., formerly Regius Professor of Divinity at the University of Oxford.

THE FIRST THREE ARGUMENTS ANSWERED

I

I take first an argument based on the statement that in founding the church's ministry Christ gave it a purely male apostolate. If, as we believe, He was God incarnate, we must surely believe that He knew what He was doing. I have heard this argument developed in various ways. He must have known, for example, of religions which had priestesses as well as priests, but did not follow that precedent. And surely, if He had thought women qualified for admission to holy orders, pride of place would have been given to His blessed mother.

These arguments ignore both the actualities of the historical situation and the meaning of the doctrine of the incarnation.

I find personally that I can best grasp the meaning of the incarnation by inventing a dialogue after the manner of the opening of the Book of Job. In this Satan says to God, "You may call yourself almighty, but there is one thing you can't do. You can't know from the inside what it is to feel, think and act like one of those human creatures of yours on the earth." The Christian doctrine of the incarnation is the belief that the earthly life of Jesus Christ was God's reply to this challenge. The reply could only be given by experiencing from the inside the life of a human individual at a particular time and place in the world's history. So Jesus was born of a Jewish mother in Palestine in the reign of Augustus Caesar and grew through the human stages of consciousness of himself as child and boy and man until he came to the conviction that he was called to be the fulfilment of God's promises to His people through the prophets to send the Messiah.

Whether or no before the crucifixion he ever thought of himself as actually God the evidence is inconclusive. His vocation as Messiah was to re-form Israel, God's chosen people, to be the instrument of His redemptive activity. For this purpose he appointed the twelve apostles as the re-formed patriarchate to take charge of the messianic community whose members, when crucified, risen and ascended, He would bind to Himself and to one another by the gift of the Holy Spirit.

In his earthly ministry his mind was moving within this Jewish circle of ideas. Christianity began as the faith of a sect of the Jews who believed that the Messiah had come in the person of Jesus, that by his death and resurrection he had won for man reconciliation with God, and by the gift of the Spirit had constituted them the members of his continuing earthly body commissioned to preach the gospel of faith in Him. How that body should grow in organisation, and in understanding of what He had been and taught and done, was left to the guidance of that same Spirit.

When we see that Jesus was concerned with the reconstitution of Israel we cease to be surprised that at that stage he did not go beyond the commissioning of the new patriarchate. He did not give instructions for gentiles to be admitted to membership on equal terms with Jews. It was not long before the church was guided by the Spirit to take that step. If we should now be being guided by the same Spirit to admit women to holy orders on the same terms as men, this would be a similar step taken likewise under the authority of the risen Lord.

Because we believe that Jesus Christ was God incarnate it is only too easy for us to read back into the gospel picture the circumstances of our own time and think of our Lord as consciously considering and deciding questions that were only to arise at later dates. In theology this corresponds to the pictorially unhistorical custom of those Italian painters who depicted gospel scenes with characters clothed in costumes of the renaissance. Arguments based on such a way of using the New Testament cannot be accepted as theologically sound.

II

I turn next to arguments based on the assumed masculinity of God and Christ. The priest has to represent God, to be a Father in God to his people. He has also to represent Christ as the Shepherd of his flock and the celebrant of the eucharist. These are essentially male activities.

When we are thinking of God in Himself, whether the unipersonal God of the Old Testament or the triune God of the Christian revelation, it is a theological mistake to think of Him as either male or female. When our spiritual ancestors first put their faith in Him as Jahweh the God of battles who rescued them from Egypt and fought for them against the Amorites and Moabites and others, they naturally thought of Him as He, and went on to look up to Him as their Father in heaven and the Husband of His chosen people. Yet He is also contrasted with the mother who forgets her child, and said to comfort Israel as one whom his mother comforteth (Isaiah 49:15; 66:13). Through prophets and psalmists He was educating them away from all this to a deeper understanding of Him as essentially the righteous, holy and loving Spirit who is the source of all that is good in creation. Those of us who try to be what the Prayer Book calls "sober, peaceable and truly conscientious sons of the Church of England" are reminded that in the first of our Articles of Religion we are called upon to think of God as "without body, parts or passions." For a Being who has no body, parts or passions, the question of sexual differentiation can have no relevance whatsoever.

Jesus Christ was undoubtedly born as man and not as woman. We have seen that for a genuine incarnation He had to experience from the inside life as a human individual. Therefore He had to be man or woman and He was made man. Again we have to take into account the historical circumstances and consider the purpose of His coming. His earthly life was lived within the circle of the Jewish religious thought of His time. He had come as Messiah to be offered in sacrifice as the Lamb of God for the taking away of the sins of the world. For this a male without blemish was required by Jewish law.

He alone could make that sacrifice, and He made it once for all. The Christian priest is not ordained to be another Christ and do again what only He could do and has done. The Christian priest has in penitence and humble thankfulness to accept for himself the benefit of that sacrifice. He is ordained to be the minister of these benefits to the other members of Christ's flock. We cannot argue from the unique circumstances of Jesus' messianic vocation that those to whom He will entrust this ministry must always be men.

I must now digress for a moment and consider how we think of holy orders. In the history of Christian theological thought there are two traditions which for convenience may be referred to as the protestant and the catholic. In the protestant tradition emphasis is laid on the thought of the ordained minister as preacher, teacher, guide and leader

127

of God's people. For the catholic the essential thing is the sacramental commissioning of the priest to pronounce absolution and celebrate the eucharist, and of the bishop to ordain.

For most of us our idea of ordination includes both sides. But the distinction can be seen from the fact that in some strongly protestant churches any member in good standing, ordained or lay, can be appointed to administer the Lord's Supper while preaching is strictly confined to the ordained. In the catholic tradition, as in the Church of England, permission to preach is freely given to laymen and laywomen but they are prohibited from pronouncing absolution or administering the sacrament of Holy Communion.

The argument from the assumed masculinity of God and Christ is especially relevant to the protestant tradition, for it thinks of the minister as representing God, the Head of the Family, or Christ, the Shepherd of the flock. It implies a further underlying assumption, that anything in the way of leadership or governance is a prerogative of the male.

The fact that this argument is used by catholic as well as protestant theologians is evidence that most of us include both sides in our idea of ordination. When St. Thomas Aquinas, for example, summarily dismisses the question of the ordination of women (without pausing to answer the awkward third point he has raised in favour of it) he does so on the ground that ordination requires in the ordinand a degree of eminence which women, being by nature in a state of subjection, do not possess.

Whence does he derive this premise? In his Herbert Spencer Lecture delivered in Oxford in 1945 on the origin of the modern use of the word science, Dr. C. E. Raven showed graphically how in biology, for example, the old bestiaries were dependent on book-learning and illustrated the traditional descriptions of animals handed down in the writings of wise men of old. The new beginning was made by men turning to the study of nature as it actually exists. It would be hard to find a better instance in support of Dr. Raven's thesis than St. Thomas' account of the nature and status of women: "The active power, as Aristotle said, is in the male semen. The woman provides the material element which has so far a vegetable kind of life. . . . This material is transformed by the power in the male semen so as to bring into existence a sensitive being." There are other passages to the same effect, in one of which it is said that this assistance in procreation is the only thing meant by the scriptural phrase "a help meet for him": all other kinds of companionship are better supplied by other men.

We should be unwise to base our theological conclusions on notions of pre-scientific biology which has never heard of genes or chromosomes.

III

Thirdly and lastly I come to an objection which is directly relevant to the catholic tradition. Ordination to the priesthood is a sacramental act, the outward and visible sign whereby is conferred the inward and spiritual grace of power to pronounce absolution and to celebrate the eucharist. The conferring of this grace is sometimes said to imprint on the recipient an indelible character. When Pope Leo XIII issued his Bull denying the validity of anglican orders the Archbishops of Canterbury and York published a Response in which they maintained that anglican ordination conferred this indelible character. The objection to the ordination of women takes the form of asserting that women are by nature incapable of receiving this indelible character.

To understand the point at issue it is necessary to realise that "indelible" and "character" are technical theological terms whose meaning is not to be derived from other uses of the words. In ordinary language "indelible" makes one think of an indelible pencil, or marking ink, the use of which so penetratingly incorporates some device in a fabric that it cannot be removed by washing; and the objection suggests that somehow or other women are so made that they cannot be so marked, as a highly sized shiny starched surface cannot be penetrated by the indelible ink. We must put all such pictures out of our minds as we turn to St. Thomas Aquinas to learn what the words mean in sacramental theology.

Take first "character." In all sacraments, says St. Thomas, it is God who acts. The human minister is commissioned by God to be the instrumental agent through whom He acts, and to enable him to do this God gives him the required spiritual potency. This spiritual potency is what is meant by character. The nature of any particular potency or character is defined by the purpose for which it is given. The character of a monetary coin is its usefulness for buying and selling. The character of a soldier is his usefulness for warfare. So the character of a priest is his potency for his use by God in absolution and the eucharist.

This sacramental character is essentially a *spiritual* potency. For St. Thomas a human being is a union of soul and flesh, of *anima* and *caro*. It is to the *anima* that the character is given, not to the *caro*. This comes out clearly in a passage in which he says that a dead priest remains a priest because it is his *caro* which is dead, not his *anima* in which the priestly character inheres.

So to say that a woman is incapable of receiving the priestly or episcopal character involves saying that her sexual differentiation carries with it a deficiency in spiritual receptivity and power. If we no longer believe that women only exist to provide the carnal material for procreation we cannot sustain an objection to their capacity for ordination on the ground of their inborn deficiency in spiritual potentiality.

What then of "indelible"? This simply means that in certain sacraments — baptism, confirmation and ordination — their grace is given once for all. They are not to be repeated. The baptised Christian may fall away from his faith, but he remains a baptised Christian. On repentance he may be restored to communion, but is not re-baptised. The priest may lose the right to exercise his character; he too when penitent may have the right restored but is not re-ordained.

Analogies from the use of indelible ink on fabrics are misleading and can only produce confusion of thought. In all our thinking about grace and sacraments we go astray if we depend on materialistic illustrations. God may make use of water, of bread and wine, of the laying on of hands, but what we are concerned with is His personal activity in His use of them. Our best clue to the meaning of "indelible" is to be found in words such as those ascribed to David in II Sam. 23:5: "God . . . hath made with me an everlasting covenant."

I have considered three types of argument which have been brought forward as theological objections to the ordination of women: those based on Christ's non-appointment of women as apostles, on the assumed masculinity of God and Christ, and on the incapacity of women to receive the sacramental character of holy orders. If the Holy Spirit, taking of the things of Christ and showing them unto us, shall lead us to see that He wills us to have women deacons, priests and bishops, I can see in none of these arguments sound theological grounds for refusing to follow His leading.[3]

ORDINATION AND SUBORDINATION
A PROBLEM IN MAN-WOMAN RELATIONSHIPS

A fourth argument often taken by those who oppose the ordination of women is based on references to the order of creation as set down in Genesis 1 and 2 and to Paul's famous dictum that women shall be silent in the churches.[4] But its essence is the assumption that God has ordained for all time the subordination of women. This view was upheld ten years ago by a Lutheran theologian, Peter Brunner. His concern is about some essential difference in the being called man and the being called woman that lies so deep in their natures that no ordinary proofs of the existence of these differences can be exhibited. To these mysterious depths only the Word of God and what he calls "the eye of the witness of Christ's resurrection" can probe. It is understandable but ominous that he uses original sin to illustrate the hiddenness and mystery of realities that lie too deep for our comprehension. But ultimately, he contends, the conflict between *being pastor* and *being woman* will reveal itself as it works itself out in the structures of culture, and he harbors a great fear that the consequences will be bad.[5]

For almost two thousand years the concept of the natural

order that spelled out the subordination of woman has held. But it is being challenged now on every hand. Brunner assumed a unanimity of opinion on subordination that is simply not a fact any more. There are indeed many clergymen, and laymen too, who are opposed to the ordination of women and would state their case in a similar way. But their number has markedly decreased in the last decade. Similarly, it is simply no longer true that as Brunner assumed there is general agreement within the Lutheran churches as to the way one distinguishes between the secular and the spiritual. This is not to argue that the church must act in agreement with the secular world; but the church must and will *respond* to the need of that world. If the church is to respond effectively, it must call upon all Christians including those who happen to be women to exercise the same basic gifts and experiences they are offering in increasing numbers to secular society. The tragedy is that, on the whole, women are simply not accustomed to looking to the church for tasks that match their abilities and training, their idealism and their desire to serve, as well as their economic needs.

There is indeed, as we have seen, strong justification for the opinion of many women who have tried to work for the church that they can render a greater service to society and meet their Christian commitments more fully *outside* the church, even though secular society has its own "orders of subordination" for women. According to Margaret Mead, the famous anthropologist, society holds so low an opinion of women who work seriously for the church, either professionally or otherwise, that it often assumes that such women are either of low mentality or victims of neuroses.[6]

The crux of the matter is in the way the church defines its ministries in the future. It seems likely that to human beings facing extinction through environmental pollution and as a result of their moral, political, economic, and social failures, the vital question will be "ordination for what?" rather than "ordination for whom?" One *has* to doubt seriously whether the ordination—whatever that is— of a woman will eventually take its toll in a negative sense. When the church has identified its ministries for our time, the problem of the ordination of women will very likely be solved in the process.

Furthermore, the discussion over the man-woman relationship is taking a new and constructive form. The old problems are still with us: male superiority, prejudice, and apprehension; female passivity and a kind of demonic reaction to an ancient woe. There will still be abrasive, paranoiac, and destructive confrontations, and we shall unquestionably hear much more of the woman's liberation movement *as revolution*. But in both the church and secular society there is a healthy and hopeful disposition to recognize that our present situation is derived from a cultural conditioning for which both sexes are responsible, and which neither society nor the church has found really creative means to correct. Both are now finally facing the fact that religions all over the world must bear responsibility for institutionalizing the subjugation of women. Both are now realizing that common distress and crises are creating new needs that will help to obliterate the ancient wrongs by making it impossible to draw distinction on any other grounds than capacity, training, and willingness to work. There is a disposition to listen to the psychologists and sociologists who point out that the differences between individuals are more weighty than the differences between the sexes when it comes to measuring capacities and gifts.

There is growing recognition of the fact that ideological Communism, which is profoundly influencing the "backward" peoples of the world, has in its own economic interest translated its ideals about the equality of the sexes into practical production. Link ideological Communism with nationalism and every society in the underdeveloped world will be shaken, veils will come off, taboos will be removed, all in the name of the common effort toward "freedom." Never mind that such emancipation may bring an "equality of the unfree." It will come anyway. The tragedy again is that a free society could not demonstrate a better road to emancipate the sexes, and that the Christian church, which for so long has believed in the sanctity of the individual (his or her *personhood*), could not somehow spell it out in its own ranks.

Let it be known, then, that certain sociological conditions all over the world have loosed political and economic forces which have meant a revolution in the status of women. The United Nations declaration of equal rights, the provisions of our civil rights laws for equality among citizens, the new freedoms for Indonesian women, Africa's drive to educate women, Israel's egalitarianism, the laws of the Communist states on marriage, divorce, and the family—are all geared to free the woman to work for the commonweal as well as for her own. Equal rights are practically a *fait accompli* and are irreversible. The traditional patriarchal forms have yielded to collective forms of life. The welfare states, for better or for worse, have been designed largely by men, and these new forms have helped to collapse the form under which the male dominated the structures of society.[7] There is already now less and less distinction between what is called "male activity" and "female activity," which is expected to result in more creative self-fulfillment for both sexes.[8]

Little publicity attends this development. Women taxi-drivers, bulldozer operators, prizefighters, meat inspectors, and croupiers get front-page treatment, but not male teachers in elementary schools, male nurses, managers of rest homes, secretaries, Girl Scout executives, chain nursery-school operators, and associate deans of students who counsel women students. American women have not paid too much attention to these changes. But the changes are profound and they are real.[9] Man needs woman as never before if the human race is to be saved.

The same point of view, with specific reference to sexual needs and the relation of sex to spiritual and intellectual development, is taken by individuals probing this aspect of the church's responsibility in marriage counseling. "Kenneth Greet, a Methodist minister, entitled his Beckley Social Service lecture for 1962, *The Mutual Society*. The phrase, as he remarks, is taken from the order of service for Christian marriage. He employs it to describe a wider and more enlightened view of sexual relations, in 'which men and women have re-examined their traditional roles, adjusted themselves to a new understanding of the truth that men and women are equal, and seen more deeply into the significance of sex itself.' "[10] The experts are telling us that men, too, desperately need to be liberated into the adventure of a full relationship with the opposite sex.

In other words, the blessings and perils of our modern society have precipitated an identity crisis for male and female alike; in the time to come the means by which they will establish their individual identities and prepare to work and live fully in this society are apt to be less sex-linked than ever before. What are often called the "crazy antics" of the hippies and the New Left with respect to "Unisex" clothing ("You can't tell the boys from the girls") and the emphasis upon hair (Why did being shorn of his hair rob Samson of his strength? Why did the French shave the heads of women who consorted with Nazi soldiers during the war?)—all of this means something.[11] But what?

135

For better or for worse the celebrated and not-so-celebrated differences between the sexes are going to be exercised in different ways in the future. The implications for the church of the drawing together of both men and women in their increasingly common tasks is obvious: positions of responsibility are to be served by persons who are judged on the basis of their competence rather than on the biological basis of sex.

It is understandable that Sigmund Freud could complain: "The great question that has never been answered and which I have not yet been able to answer, despite my thirty years of research into the feminine soul is this: 'What does woman want?' " What is less understandable is that Freud could not see that this problem is not woman's alone; it is man's and mankind's. There are two easy ways out of the dilemma: one is to take the Muhammadan position that women have no souls; the other is to say that it was all settled in the Garden of Eden. The Christian can accept neither position. The rejection of the first is obvious; the rejection of the second is valid if one believes that the Creator is still at work and that redemption is not only an act but a process as well.[12]

In the pamphlet, *A Study of the Man-Woman Relationship,* published in 1952 for the Commission on the Life and Work of Women of the Church of the World Council of Churches, there is a profound and provocative treatment of the idea that ". . . there is a tension between an order of creation 'male and female made He them' and an order of redemption 'in Christ there is neither male nor female.' " Was Christ ". . . the archetype of a fully united humanity and not of masculine humanity alone?" Are we at a point in human development where the church can speak more precisely of redemption *within* the society? "Many Christians feel that churches have no sense of the

136

urgency of showing how our present-day situation in man-woman relationships can be redeemed. Meanwhile in secular society various groups are trying to work out a pattern of redemption in man-woman relationships, looking both to science and to their own partial understanding of the gospel for help."[13] But now, seventeen tumultuous years later, the atmosphere is far more receptive to elevated, sober, and productive discussion on man-woman relationships within the church.[14]

Ordination remains, then, in the minds of most Lutherans, Anglicans, Roman Catholics, and Orthodox clergy, the most controversial and the most threatening of all problems. No matter at what point the discussion of the woman question begins, sooner or later the subject of ordination arises. (It is a disaster that the word "subordination," and the conditions and feelings it invokes, follows so closely on the heels of "ordination.") Although the pressures for the ordination of women have been strong among many Protestant groups in Europe and even among Catholic women's groups in Europe and America, no such organized efforts have been made by Protestant women in the United States. Part of the reason is, of course, that most American churches permit ordination. Here and there a lone woman or two appears ready to make a test case upon graduating from a theological seminary. More test cases are expected. But generally women who wish to work for the church do not make a great point of insisting upon ordination. The crux of the matter is justice, and the major complaint is that traditionally the church has gone along with society in treating women as inferior human beings and stunting their ability to exploit their gifts to the fullest. To be barred from ordination perpetuates this tradition whose theological supports are at least questionable. Their position is roughly analogous to that of the Negro in the open-housing issue: "We don't necessarily *want* to live among whites. We know the problems. But we should be free to choose." The few women who are firmly pressing for this right, however, feel very strongly about it, primarily as a cause that must be fought for.

THE PROBLEM OF ECUMENICITY

There is no question but that the "woman problem" poses a threat to ecumenical fellowship between Protestants and the Roman Catholic and Orthodox churches, and between other Protestant churches and the Anglican communion. Pulpit and altar fellowship between the Anglicans and the Swedish Lutherans, based primarily upon their common belief in apostolic succession, has been threatened by the ordination of women by the Swedish church. Fellowship between the more "liberal" Lutheran churches and the Lutheran Church—Missouri Synod is threatened as well. Three factors are powerfully at work, however. First, there is a grass-roots revolt within the Roman Catholic Church which emphasizes the view that other points of division than ordination of women are far more substantive. Should the Lutheran Church in America take this step, it would probably evoke explosive protests from the conservative prelates of the Catholic church and nods of approval from liberal theologians, who, after all, are most active in establishing an ecumenical dialog. In time, as the cultural tide carries the role of women in new directions, a climate of acceptance would probably prevail. Second, the contemporary crises in all the churches may quite simply force a bona fide and practical cooperation among them to the point where this particular threat of women usurping functions traditionally assigned to males will seem irrelevant or at least fall to a much lower level on the critical list.

Stranger developments than these are likely to occur within the foreseeable future. In their anxiety about ecumenism, Lutherans would do well to remember that more than half of all Lutherans in the world belong to churches that have already ordained women.

The third factor has to do with development within the world picture of the ecumenical movement. Remarkable contributions are being made by women's organizations to the cause of ecumenical fellowship. It is ironic that Catholic and Protestant women all over the world have been moved to a vibrant and productive ecumenism partly because they have not been taken seriously by their own churches. The World Council of Churches has with great imagination seized upon this fact of life and established a Department on Cooperation of Men and Women in Church, Family, and

---

MEN, WOMEN, AND ECUMENISM—WCC STATEMENT

The confrontation of different churches has proved to be very fruitful. Clearly there is no question of trying to formulate uniform answers and describing in the abstract what men and women should be and do today. One cannot preach what the Bible tells us about the nature of man and woman, nor make use of biological or psychological data, without reference to a definite sociological context. The Christian life cannot be lived, nor a social problem answered, in the same way in Finland as in the U.S., in Moslem Algeria as in Buddhist Thailand, in over-populated and highly-industrialized Japan as in the Congo, in Russia, Brazil or Indonesia. But it is essential to share experiences, the valuable fruit of so many different situations. These exchanges help to distinguish more clearly between what is fundamental and inherent in Christianity, and what is conditioned by the times, by economic or social conditions or by a particular culture.

The questions concerning changes in the respective roles

of man and woman are particularly urgent for the churches of Asia, Africa, and the South Sea Islands. They need to rethink the teaching and the way of life brought by missionaries and to find their own Christian way. They must distinguish between what is merely Western and can be rejected, and what is fundamentally Christian and thus universally valid. They must at the same time reexamine their own cultures and traditions, in order to discover what can be preserved and what is incompatible with the Christian life.

But these questions are equally essential for the churches which have a long tradition behind them. They see their institutions crumbling, their systems of thought once considered unchangeable are disintegrating. They, too, must help their members and the society to which they belong to rediscover new ways of living and thinking.

It is for the World Council of Churches to transmit faithfully the most divergent opinions, just as it must make known the points on which a common opinion exists or is coming into being. This common opinion may be the starting point of other consensuses, and so become a contribution towards the unity of Christians and their common service to the world.[15]

Society ". . . deliberately different from the 'Commissions on Women's Questions' or the 'Women's Departments' which have traditionally brought women together and left them on their own to confront problems arising from their changing roles—problems which in fact concern men just as much as women."[16]

Hope is bright that a redefinition of the ministries of the church in our time will bring with it the wisdom to identify the rites by which the church recognized its ministers in such a way that the "most delicate matter" of women and ordination may well be subsumed under matters that are much more pressing for the whole community of God's people.

NOTES

1. Leonard Hodgson, *Theological Objections to the Admission of Women to Holy Orders,* p. 1.

2. Ibid., p. 2.

3. Ibid., pp. 2-8.

4. See above, pp. 13-18.

5. Peter Brunner, "The Ministry and the Ministry of Women," *Lutheran World,* December 1959, pp. 270, 272.

6. Cassara, ed., *American Women,* p. xii.

7. Hahn, *Partnership,* p. 6.

8. See Aaron L. Rutledge, "Male and Female Roles in Marriage Counseling," *Pastoral Psychology,* October 1962, p. 10.

9. James B. Ashbrook, "The Church as a Matriarchy," *Pastoral Psychology,* September 1963, pp. 38-49.

10. Ludovici, *The Final Inequality,* p. 27.

11. We do not mean to imply that all of this makes sense. The "woman problem" has split the ranks of the New Left and other radical groupings. For instance, Stokely Carmichael on one occasion summed up SNCC's attitude, crudely but succinctly, thus: "The only position for women in SNCC is prone!" Many young women who have worked for SDS long and hard have been so insulted and injured by being ignored by policy-making units while they typed, printed, folded, and stamped, that they have left the movement. They asserted, logically enough, that if there was not freedom for women in a movement dedicated to freeing minority groups, there could be no freedom eventually for anyone. In a bizarre and striking fashion a group of Antioch students supported the new liberation movement for women by appearing nude before a visiting parcel of men from *Playboy* magazine to demonstrate their rejection of the *Playboy* attitude toward women and sex.

12. "Whenever the church's message is determined exclusively by Gen. 3:1 ff., the fall of man, it underestimates the human possibilities given to the first Adam and restored by the second Adam, and its influence is negated by harsh legalism." George Forell, "Christian Freedom and Religious Liberty," *Lutheran Quarterly,* November 1964, p. 333.

13. World Council of Churches, *A Study of the Man-Woman Relationship,* pp. 20, 26.

14. For a summary of the record of the Western churches, see the reports of the World Council of Churches surveys on the ordination of women in 1953 and 1963. The substance of them is in Culver, *Women in the World of Religion,* Appendix III, pp. 289-293. See also the *Christian Century,* April 20, 1966, p. 502.

15. Barot, *Cooperation of Men and Women in Church, Family and Society,* pp. 10, 11.

16. Ibid., p. 2.

Chapter 11

The Diaconate

As we move into the 1970s it is obvious that the rediscovery of the New Testament concept of *diakonia,* which led to the creation of varying kinds of orders for deacons and deaconesses in the nineteenth century, will converge with the much more drastic twentieth-century emphasis upon the church serving society to effect drastic changes in the diaconate.[1] The problem is already upon all the churches, and the signs of change abundantly clear.[2] They are to be seen in the turmoil within the Catholic clergy and especially, of course, the laity. A diaconate for men was set up by the Vatican in 1967 and approved by the Catholic bishops in the United States in November 1968. The first married deacon was ordained to his office in June 1969. Meanwhile, four centers in the United States have been established where candidates may take a two-year course of preparation. The deacon may serve as parish pastor, preach, baptize, distribute Holy Communion, and officiate at weddings and funerals. He may not say mass.[3]

The Anglican and Presbyterian churches are also seeking to bring the laity and the clergy closer together by a new definition of the authority, duties, and status of the deacon. Those churches which have long since settled upon a vocabulary that designates "deacon" as male and the "diaconate" as female—especially the Lutheran churches—are under pressure to clarify their understanding of the *diakonia* as they have institutionalized it. One Lutheran deaconess emphasized the deep frustrations experienced by the present form of the diaconate and urged upon the church the need ". . . to find new ways and means to refresh and reequip its members to be better servants in the church and to experience a more meaningful personal life. . . . The future of the diaconate in the Lutheran Church in America seems to be illusive. I see no clear-cut direction for it." [4]

In response to the rising demand for a broad study of the contemporary status of the *diakonia,* an Ecumenical Secretariat for the Diaconal Ministry of the Church was established in Geneva as a three-year experiment. It is sponsored by the World Federation of Deaconess Associations and the Federation for Inner and Christian Social Work, in cooperation with the World Council of Churches. One of its projects was to hold a consultation between the Ecumenical Secretariat and the Roman Catholic Information Center's special body for diaconal affairs in Switzerland in the fall of 1968. A summary of the discussions by Dr. Lukas Vischer and other reports from different churches point out that the traditional structure of the church has not given adequate expression to its diaconal responsibility. The Reverend Bengt-Thure Molander, executive secretary of the Ecumenical Secretariat, expressed the need of the churches in their renewal to become "a diaconal church . . ., or it will not be the Church."

MOLANDER ON THE DIACONAL CHURCH

At a time in history when the world is in deep crisis and in a process of renewal, the old structures of the churches themselves questioned and often felt obsolete, no fruitful research as to the specificity and function of the Ministry of Deacons can be pursued in isolation. It must be part of the great reappraisal and research for renewal which the churches themselves and the ministry in general must

143

undergo. The Church must become a diaconal Church in the deepest and most foreward-looking sense, or it will not be the Church. It is therefore important, in this diaconal perspective, that our churches meet and challenge one another theologically, in a true ecumenical spirit. It is also important that the new needs of our times should challenge our churches, their theology and ministry. Only as these two currents influence one another can we be lead to see what structures and ministries the churches really need. . . . Meanwhile in this process of renewal, the deacon and the deaconess by their presence, by the questions they pose to the Church, are reminders of the full diaconal dimension of the Churches' Ministry and should be incitements and not impediments to renewal.[5]

Three organizations of deaconesses are currently discussing the issues involved in the new diaconate that seems to be emerging and anticipating the implications for them as women.[6] The World Federation of Deaconess Associations, organized in 1947 in Copenhagen, now includes deaconess organizations from twenty-one countries and represents about thirty-five thousand deaconesses. The tenth meeting of this ecumenical organization took place in 1969 in Tampere, Finland, with about five hundred delegates and visitors present. The North American Deaconesses Organization held its first conference in Racine, Wisconsin, in 1968 and drew about one hundred delegates from nine denominational churches into a discussion of the role of the diaconate in a radically changing society. The Lutheran Deaconess Conference, representing all Lutheran churches in North America, has been meeting every two years since 1896 and is the oldest inter-Lutheran organization of America. The deaconesses of the Missouri Synod joined the conference in 1968.

The women of the churches of all denominations have, consciously or unconsciously, voted their reactions to the problems of the diaconate and their confidence in its future for them by refusing to be recruited into this service of the church in significant numbers.

In the opinion of Sister Anna Ebert, of the Lutheran Church in America, the following questions require consideration:

1. If the church is primarily to be understood as the people of God and the ministry is there solely for the strengthening of the people of God, how should the diaconal ministry be related to the priestly or pastoral ministry? Can it be a ministry among equal ministries and understood as each carrying out specific functions?
2. Just as there appear to be no scriptural or theological reasons for limiting the ordained ministry to men, is there any reason for continuing to limit the diaconate to women in the LCA? With the diaconate open to men and women, then its assignment can be more meaningful as "diaconal stimulators or enablers" in the church to enable God's people to fulfill their diaconal tasks.
3. Is there any merit in considering the diaconate as the office embracing the present diversity of professional church workers, e.g., directors of Christian education, social workers, teachers, with the present LCA deaconess community as one of its forms? [7]
4. Since worship is the source from which *diakonia* arises and *diakonia* without worship is empty, what can be done to strengthen their relationship in a more effective manner to dramatize the responsibility of God's people to be a church-for-others? Is the honest recognition of a diaconate part of the answer?

In short, the winds of change are blowing. The new world, the new church, the new woman are bearing down upon the ancient institution of the diaconate to bring it to new life.

NOTES

1. For a brief history of the diaconate since the early church, see above pp. 18-24.

2. For a study of the problems of the diaconate in general, as well as a report on the state of the diaconate in the Orthodox Church and several Protestant churches, see *The Ministry of Deacons* (Geneva: World Council of Churches, 1965). See also the World Council of Churches, *The Role of the Diakonia of the Church in Contemporary Society* (Geneva, 1966).

3. *The Lutheran*, July 2, 1969, p. 27.

4. Comment from a commission interview.

5. Introduction to "The Ministry of Deacons" (a report on the consultation), *Diakonia News,* January 1969, p. 2.

6. Sister Anna Ebert, of the Lutheran Church in America, furnished much of the information on the structure and organization of the diaconal orders presented here.

7. The same idea was expressed by Dr. Lukas Vischer in *The Ministry of Deacons,* p. 7: ". . . the diaconate can assume a great variety of forms. If the diaconate is to be renewed at the present time, we need to have the imagination that is capable of finding new forms. In all Churches, thinking is burdened by precedents. They are inadequate and unsatisfactory."

Chapter 12

Present and
Future Directions

WOMEN AND CIVIL RIGHTS

Just how to relate the role of women in the church with the civil rights movement in which many of the churches are deeply involved is one of the many logistical, moral, and theological problems precipitated by the women's liberation movement. It is obvious that the movement has helped to crystallize this discontent, but the church women's problem is different in essence and in purpose.

Much of the discussion of the woman problem is freighted by three things, in themselves valid and relevant, but not of commanding importance here. First, the mounting discontent and frustration of women within the church is generating the same kind of fervor and crusading spirit that marked the "bloomer" and suffragette movements of the nineteenth and early twentieth centuries, which elicited fifty years of humiliating and frivolous response before women finally received voting rights. Anyone who doubts that the automatic male (and much female) response to the effort of women to gain civil rights is irresponsible and outrageous would do well to read the floor debate on Title VII of the Civil Rights Act.[1] Another millstone is provided by the use of the word "equal." There is nothing absolute about equality and the efforts to guarantee it by law in the name of justice cannot be fully effective. It is good that we have a public school system, but a single person pays relatively much more to support it than the father of eight children who benefit by it. The outlook must be broader and embrace a great many imponderable factors. The Christian finds equality an anemic word indeed to describe the promise of creation for him as an *individual person* and as a child of God. On this imperfect earth, however, the Christian is committed to see that his imperfect institutions, his imperfect traditions, his imperfect vocabulary do not bind another human being in such a way as to prevent him from realizing as much of his or her potential as possible. Meanwhile, within its own structures and in such practical matters as salaries, fringe benefits, promotions, and tests and judgments on competence, the church must abide by the law, which with all *its* imperfections honestly seeks what we call "equality." Otherwise, the church in violating its own principles will inevitably tangle with the law.[2]

A third factor which burdens the discussion of the woman problem is the similarity between the woman's liberation movement and the black revolution. The first ranks behind the second in civic concern and surprisingly enough in the churches as well. For instance, a well-known church magazine recently carried two pieces, side by side. In the first article the church was urged to go forward in its support of the Negro cause. In the next, the church was urged to exercise great caution in supporting larger responsibilities for women in the church because of the threat to inter-church relations.

Both women and black people in the job market face handicaps. "Both are fired before white men and hired after them. Both are arbitrarily limited to the lower-paying, least productive, less-skilled jobs and sometimes the same ones. . . . The gap between the races in job tenure is similar to the gap between the sexes. . . . Neither Negroes nor white women gravitate to steady work. Both are fired before white men, of course, but both are more apt to quit because they move away or can't get transportation to the job. Women and Negroes often do not have as much control over where they live as white men." [3] The church should take notice of the similarities in order to eliminate prejudice. It should, however, keep its eye upon the ultimate concern of the Christian, which includes the conviction that the woman as an individual on this earth must be free within the communion of saints to serve the God who created and redeemed her and placed her in that community.

THE FEMINIZATION OF THE CHURCH

It has been noted with increasing alarm and over a long period of time that women have been numerically more prominent in the congregation at worship and in serving the church and society than their fellow male Christians. The Church of Scotland is unhappy because a recent survey revealed that 65 percent of recruits under twenty-one and 53 percent of those over twenty-one were women. The alarm is mixed with relief, however, for there is an acknowledged tendency to allow women to be nominated as candidates for church councils simply because no male candidates could be found. It is feared by some that a feminization of the clergy may take place for the same reasons. If the feminization of the church *for whatever reason* takes place as society moves inevitably toward some resolution of its dilemmas, there *may* be some blessing in it. (The elevation of the Virgin Mary resulted in the building of Chartres cathedral as well as compensating at long last for the overmasculinization of the church.)

The one way out of this dilemma is to turn away from the male-female confrontation stance and make the team relationship as effective as possible. It is theologically sound

and eminently practical, and now in a time of great flux
filled with enormous possibilities for the church.

"MALE BACKLASH"

Inevitably and understandably, the increasing stridency
and the stepped-up tempo of the more aggressive elements
in the woman's liberation movement have evoked strong
responses. "This thing is getting out of hand," is an opinion
of many liberals who are fundamentally in favor of the
fuller use of woman power in every facet of life—including
the church. This reaction is a tendency in all reform and
revolutionary movements. The contemporary drives to "po-
larize" society on all issues will aggravate the problem.
This polarization of the sexes has taken place in radical
groups of both the right and the left, and a male backlash
is shaping up.[4]

The problem is mentioned simply because as the church
struggles to define its ministries to its own people and to
society, it must recognize that the images of what is male
and what is female are changing and that the battle between what has been traditional and what is already happening has begun. The church's task is to recognize that
the conflict exists, to understand it, and to elevate it to
creative purposes that are consonant with what we conceive to be God's purposes.

NEW DIRECTIONS

What now is to be done?

1. Let us face the historical fact that the church itself
has helped to perpetuate an image of woman that has been
derived from ancient cultures and is on the whole deroga-
tory and destructive and that the consequences of this tradi-

tion are depriving both women and men of their full potential in their relations with one another, the family, society, and the church.

2. Let us face the theological implications of the fact that the Christ who called his people into new life on this earth did not lay down rigid rules of order, but a principle of love which was to be the wellspring of that new life and the only guarantee that authority and order shall prevail to strengthen the church to do its task.

3. Let us draw upon the findings of the psychologists and sociologists who say that only experience in our time and in our circumstances can identify those spheres of activity which belong to women and those which do not and admit that it is wrong to deprive women and society of the opportunity to have this experience.

4. Let us recognize that women are already proving themselves in a great variety of tasks within and outside the church; let us hold the door open to experimentation and act upon the knowledge that both men and women have latent gifts that develop under new conditions and new tasks.

5. Let us, in this spirit of creative experimentation:
   a. Explore the possibilities of team ministries.
   b. Test the willingness of some congregations, in the traditional parish form as well as in experimental ministries, to accept the services of professionally educated women.
   c. Accept a broader and deeper concept of the diaconate which will in worship and in work, in diaconate communities and outside them, call upon the laity to minister to one another and to society.
   d. Explore the possibilities of part-time paid and unpaid diaconal-type services for both men and women who are qualified for work on behalf of

the church in institutions such as hospitals, schools, and factories.

e. Explore the possibilities of recruitment and educational programs that will assist women to escape the barrenness of social, economic, and religious structures that stymie the growth of the spirit and reduce existence either to drudgery or frivolity.

f. Study the resources of our colleges and seminaries (their curricula, their recruitment practices, their counseling procedures, their facilities, and all matters pertinent to the development of career possibilities for women in the total life of the church) to see whether women students are given opportunities and encouragement equal to that of men students.

g. Establish a permanent commission, with men and women members, authorized to conduct the investigations and initiate the programs mentioned above and to experiment with others, as the work of the church may require in a new age.

6. Keep our ears open to the Holy Spirit who speaks to us in every age.

NOTES

1. Caroline Bird gives a good account of this debate in her excellent book, *Born Female.*

2. The *New York Times* of August 10, 1969, carried a story dealing with "a battle of the sexes" in Clark County, Nevada, which includes Las Vegas. Women wanted to be candidates for jobs as croupiers in the gambling casinos. Men were resisting on the grounds that family men and veterans would be replaced and "that employers would try to hire good-looking girls to attract men to play the games. The customers would flirt with the girls and not concentrate on the dealing." It doesn't take a dirty mind to make a comparison with the rule in some Lutheran and Catholic churches that women may clean the church buildings but not the altar, or the priestly rule that a nun may assist at certain services, but may not stand or serve near the priest

or go beyond the railing on the grounds that she may not only corrupt the holy place but distract the other servant of God. The two cases are comparable only in their implications for *womanhood*, but in certain cases of professional services within the church, civil rights action may eventually have to be faced.

3. Bird with Briller, *Born Female*, p. 141.

4. See, for instance, reports on the SDS as a masculine movement; the review of Cayo Sexton's book, *The Feminized Male*, in the *Saturday Review*, August 16, 1969; the advertisement in the *Saturday Review*, April 26, 1969, p. 83, for a summer session for apathetic students under "expert *male* faculty"; the advertisements for Dr. Bruno Bettleheim's book, *The Children of the Dream*, which traces many problems in children to the American woman torn between independence and maternal demands and points to the kibbutz experience as a corrective; and Lionel Tiger's book, *Men in Groups*, whose thesis is that society's survival depends more crucially upon man's affinity for man than on his reproductive affinity for women, and that when ". . . a community deals with its most vital problems . . . females do not participate. The public forum is a male forum" (quoted from a review in *Time*, June 20, 1969).

Bibliography

Bibliography

Barot, Madeleine. *Cooperation of Men and Women in Church, Family and Society*. Geneva: World Council of Churches, 1964.

Bird, Caroline, with Briller, Sara Welles. *Born Female: The High Cost of Keeping Women Down*. New York: David McKay, 1968.

Bührig, Marga. "Position of Women in the Church." *The Educated Woman*, a special issue of *Student World*, no. 3, 1966.

Cassara, Beverly Benner, ed. *American Women: The Changing Image*. Boston: Beacon Press, 1962.

Central Advisory Council for the Ministry of the Church Assembly. *Gender and the Ministry*. Oxford: Church Army Press, 1962.

Church of England, commission appointed by the archbishops of Canterbury and York. *Women and Holy Orders*. The Central Board of Finance, Church of England, 1966.

Culver, Elsie Thomas. *Women in the World of Religion*. New York: Doubleday, 1967.

Daly, Mary. "Built-in Bias." *Commonweal*, January 15, 1965.

————. *The Church and the Second Sex*. New York: Harper and Row, 1968.

Devaux, André A. *Teilhard and Womanhood*. Glen Rock, New Jersey: Paulist Press, Deus Books, 1968.

Dumas, Francine. *Man and Woman: Similarity and Difference*. Geneva: World Council of Churches, 1966.

Friedan, Betty. *The Feminine Mystique*. New York: W. W. Norton, 1963.

Gruberg, Martin. *Women in American Politics: An Assessment and Sourcebook*. New York: Academic Press, 1968.

Hahn, Elisabeth. *Partnership*. Geneva: World Council of Churches Commission on the Life and Work of Women in the Church, 1954.

Hefner, Philip J. "Ministry of Women." *Lutheran Quarterly,* May 1966, pp. 101-103.

Hodgson, Leonard. *Theological Objections to the Admission of Women to Holy Orders.* Cambridge: R. I. Severs, 1967.

Kaesemann, Ernest. *Essays on New Testament Themes, Studies in Biblical Theology, No. 41.* London: SCM Press, 1964.

Lampe, G. W. H. *The Church's Tradition and the Question of Ordination of Women to the Historic Ministry.* Cambridge: R. I. Severs, 1967.

Lamson, Peggy. *Women in Political Life Today.* Boston: Houghton Mifflin, 1968.

Lauer, Rosemary. "Women Clergy for Rome?" *Christian Century,* September 14, 1966.

Lewis, Edwin C. *Developing Woman's Potential.* Ames, Iowa: Iowa State University Press, 1968.

Lifton, Robert Jay. *The Woman in America.* Boston: Houghton Mifflin, 1965.

Lindbeck, Violette S. "Should We Ordain Women?" *Salt,* vol. 4, no. 1, spring, 1967.

Ludovici, Laurence James. *The Final Inequality.* New York: W. W. Norton, 1965.

Lutheran Church in America, Report of the Commission on the Comprehensive Study of the Doctrine of the Ministry, Appendix A, "Women in the Ministry of the Church." *Minutes of the Third Biennial Convention.* Philadelphia: Lutheran Church in America, 1966.

McGovern, James. "The American Woman's Pre-World War I Freedom in Manners and Morals." *Journal of American History,* September 1968, pp. 316–333.

McKenna, Sister Mary Laurence. *Women of the Church.* New York: P. J. Kenedy & Sons, 1967.

President's Commission on the Status of Women. *American Women.* New York: Charles Scribner's Sons, 1965.

Prohl, Russell C. *Woman in the Church.* Grand Rapids, Michigan: Eerdmans, 1957.

Rensenbrink, Dorothy. "On Their Way Together: Update on Church Women United." *Tempo,* August 1, 1969.

Reuther, Rosemary. "The Becoming of Women in Church and Society." *Cross Currents,* fall, 1967.

Ryrie, Charles Caldwell. *The Place of Women in the Church.* New York: Macmillan, 1958.

Shannon, Margaret. "CWU and the Women Liberators." *Tempo,* August 1, 1969.

Stendahl, Krister. *The Bible and the Role of Women: A Case Study in Hermeneutics.* Philadelphia: Fortress Press, 1966.

Thrall, M. E. *The Ordination of Women to the Priesthood. A Study of the Biblical Evidence.* London: SCM Press, 1958.

Way, Peggy. "Women in the Church." *Renewal,* October 1964, pp. 4–8.

Wedel, Cynthia. "Church Women and Christian Unity." *Catholic World,* February 1966.

―――. *Employed Women and the Church.* New York: National Council of the Churches of Christ in the United States of America, 1959.

Wilson, Charles Morrow. "The Case of the Multiplying Women Preachers." *Modern Age,* fall 1969.

The Woman in America, the spring 1964 issue of *Daedalus: The Journal of the American Academy of Arts and Sciences.* The Proceedings of the American Academy of Arts and Sciences, vol. 93, no. 2.

"Women in the Church: A Theological Problem?" *The Ecumenist,* 1965.

World Council of Churches Commission on the Life and Work of Women in the Church. *A Study of the Man-Woman Relationship.* London: SCM Press, 1952.

World Council of Churches Department on Cooperation of Men and Women in Church, Family and Society, and the Faith and Order Commission. *Concerning the Ordination of Women.* Geneva, 1964.

Zerbst, Fritz. *The Office of Woman in the Church.* St. Louis: Concordia Publishing House, 1955.

Type, 10 on 12 and 9 on 10 Caledonia and 9 on 10 Futura
Display, Americana and Futura